OUR DOCTRINES

Methodist Theology as Classical Christianity

KENNETH CRACKNELL

CLIFF COLLEGE
PUBLISHING

CLIFF COLLEGE PUBLISHING
Cliff College, Calver, Hope Valley,
Nr Sheffield S32 3XG

ISBN 1 898362 19 X

Data conversion, Typesetting, Cover Design
& Production Management:

MOORLEY'S Print & Publishing
23 Park Rd., Ilkeston, Derbys DE7 5DA
Tel/Fax: (0115) 932 0643

Printed & Bound at Redwood Books

Preface

An invitation to give the annual lecture on 'Classical Christianity' under the auspices of Cliff College during the Methodist Conference in Scarborough in 1998 has given me the opportunity to set out some of my deepest convictions. I am most grateful to Principal Howard Mellor for thus provoking me to give reasons why Methodist theology is neither to be understood as dependent upon, nor to be judged by, some notion called 'classical Christianity'. On the contrary, I argue that both the doctrines and the practices of Methodism (to be sure, when they are seen at their best) may justly be interpreted as accurate and appropriate expressions of historical Christianity. I have also come to believe that many of the insights and emphases of Methodism are essential to ecumenical and interfaith dialogue, and need therefore to be recaptured and revitalized.

Living now as I do in the U.S.A., I am aware as never before that there is a veritable torrent of new writing and reflection to support such a position. Much of what follows is dependent upon the theological renaissance now taking place among North American Methodist scholars, and the extensive bibliographical footnotes of this little book will, I hope, take many readers into new and illuminating territory.

My own students from Wesley House, Cambridge, from 1988 to 1995, will recognize many themes that we explored together in our Ministry and Mission classes: the value of the doctrinal clause in the 1932 Deed of Union; the theological importance of *Wesley's Forty Four Sermons* and the *Explanatory Notes on the New Testament*; the significance for church life of hymnody (and disastrous consequences of bad hymnody); the distillation of Wesleyan theology in two key phrases, 'evangelical Ar-

3

minianism' and 'the optimism of grace', and the vital relevance of the conception of 'prevenient grace' to all aspects of Christian mission: to evangelism, to social action, to pastoral care, and to life in a religiously plural world.

Such themes make up 'a Gospel to proclaim'. My hope now is that this small contribution may be part of widespread renewal of confidence in 'our doctrines' and thus lead to a revitalization of our preaching and teaching.

Saffron Walden,
June 1998   KENNETH CRACKNELL

4

Kenneth Cracknell is Director of Global Studies and Research Professor in Theology and Mission at Brite Divinity
School, Texas Christian University, Fort Worth, Texas.
Before going to the USA, he held the Michael C. Gut-
teridge Chair of Systematic and Pastoral Theology at
Wesley House, Cambridge where he was also President of
the Cambridge Theological Federation. He has also served
as Executive Secretary for Relationships with People of
Other Faiths at the former British Council of Churches, in
pastoral ministry in Loughborough, Leicestershire, and as
a missionary educator in Nigeria.

Chapter One:
What is Classical Christianity?

From the beginnings of the Wesleyan movement candidates for the ministry have been examined in 'our doctrines'. The possessive pronoun suggests a self-conscious sense of 'distinctiveness' of special emphases delivered to John Wesley and his followers, perhaps even of new insights into the ancient deposit of the faith. Yet no one was more emphatic than Wesley himself that his teaching was but 'Primitive Christianity', as received by the best authorities in all the ages and as especially to be found in the formularies of the Anglican Church. His Methodism was to be 'the old religion, the religion of the Bible, the religion ... of the Primitive Church, the religion of the Church of England',[1] Sectarian or schismatic doctrines were to him the very curse of the Devil. So what is going on in the words of my title? Is there anything indeed truly distinctive in Methodist teaching to warrant the use of the expression 'our doctrines'?

Perhaps there is not, and nor, in one sense should there be. Methodists after all are not to be distinguished in doctrine from all other descendants of the Protestant Reformation. In the nineteenth century candidates for the ministry were examined, according to contemporary manuals 'in the great verities of our natural depravity, repentance, justification, adoption, the witness of the Spirit, entire sanctification, and the mutual relations of all these both as revealed truth and as experimental facts.' Except for the

---

[1]   *At the Foundation of City Road Chapel*, Jackson's *Works*, vol.7, cf. 'It is the one old religion; as old as the Reformation; as old as Moses; as old as Adam.' quoted in R.S. Chiles, *Theological Development in American Methodism, 1790-1935*, University Press of America, 1983, p. 84.

reference to entire sanctification there is nothing particularly 'ours' about that list. The curriculum and syllabus material of the theological training institutions in Britain and in the USA, as well as of the textbooks produced by the tutors and professors, show that the broad patterns of Protestant theology were the staple fare. Thomas Jackson at Richmond, for example, taught as much from the Puritan divines as he did from any particular Methodist source. The two greatest of the Wesleyan systematic theologies of the nineteenth century, the *Theological Institutes* (1823) of Richard Watson (1781-1833) and the *Compendium of Christian Theology* by William Burt Pope (1822-1903) are remarkable for their conformity to contemporary Protestant patterns of going about this task. To be sure Watson intended to be neither 'Calvinistic' nor 'Pelagian', and thus a good Wesleyan, but he was much more committed to expounding 'the theological system of the Holy Scriptures' in the face of rationalist doubtings. Pope likewise wrote three massive volumes on God, Sin and Redemption, and on the Administration of Redemption viewed, according to his subtitle, as Biblical, Dogmatic, Historical. Of the three basic divisions only the last was deemed by Pope to touch on the 'peculiarities of Methodist theology'. For the rest Pope lays under tribute the theologians of the great tradition of the Church. Methodist theology, he wrote, is 'Catholic in the best sense, holding the Doctrinal Articles of the English Church including the three Creeds, and therefore maintaining the general doctrine of the Reformation.' [2] As the century wore on theologians on both sides of the Atlantic were increasingly concerned with the challenges to Christian doctrine arising chiefly from science and psychology, but also from the new discoveries in the field of comparative religion. As a result the long reign

---

[2]   *Compendium of Christian Theology*, Wesleyan Conference Office, 2nd edn 1879, Vol. 1. p. 20.

of Richard Watson in the USA came to an end and American Methodists began to diverge very considerably from Wesleyan norms. In his valuable survey *Theological Development in American Methodism,* Robert Chiles traces three stages in this progressive divergence. First, American Methodist theology became a form of 'liberal evangelicalism', a type of 'evangelical liberalism' and then gave itself almost entirely to meeting the demands of interpreting Christ to the contemporary culture. In this last stage, Methodist theologians, like other mainstream denominational thinkers, in Chiles's words, 'pleasantly bade good-bye to their predecessors.'[3]

In the same manner British Methodists conformed to the general patterns of theological reflection, and it would be hard to specify what was distinctively Methodist in, for example, the preaching of John Scott Lidgett, W.E. Sangster, Leslie Weatherhead or Donald Soper.[4] This was so much the case that by 1959 the cumulative effect of the papers presented at the first Oxford Methodist Theological Institute led Henry Rack to comment that when dissentions occurred among Methodist theologians, these 'reflected Barthian, Liberal, Biblical-theological and Existentialist points of view'. As Rack says there was nothing specifically Methodist about these.[5] That fine scholar of the last generation, Rupert Davies, may be taken to illustrate this point. His book, *What Methodists Believe* could equally

---

[3]   *Op.cit.* p. 66.

[4]   The greatest Methodist preacher in Britain in the early part of the century, J. Scott Lidgett wrote in these terms: 'Wesley inherited the great tradition of New Testament, Catholic and Reformed theology. He accepted its doctrines, emphasised their meaning, and for the most part moved within their boundaries. Yet the quality of "newness" extends beyond "new ideas". There may be a new emphasis, a new proportion, a recovery of what has been neglected and become obscure, which may effect as true and vital a revolution as the importation of new ideas from without. Such newness was characteristic of Wesley's teaching.' *The Idea of God and Social Ideals,* p. 82.

[5]   Henry Rack, *The Future of John Wesley's Methodism,* Lutterworth and James Knox Press, 1965, p. 54.

well have been entitled *What Christians Believe,* for only in the last chapter does he turn to Methodist distinctives [6]

His colleague Gordon Rupp presumably felt much the same. Henry Rack quotes him as remarking that 'what is really distinctive about Methodism, is not particular bits and pieces of doctrine, some of which have come to be shared with other churches, but rather a particular history'. Presumably much in agreement with Rupp, Rack continues: 'If so, this is a history made up of a particular blend of traditions, and inherited ethos and way of behaviour, the remains of a vision of a people pursuing inward religion in company rather than alone, informally rather than formally'.[7]

But Davies, Rupp and Rack are historians, not systematic theologians.[8] On the other side of the Atlantic a new thing was happening, somewhat unbeknown to British Methodists, a new generation of systematic theologians was beginning to take Wesley seriously as a theologian. Since these people are all actively at work reconstructing the grand contours of Wesley's theological achievement, it is inappropriate to name any names but one.[9] This is the name of Albert Outler (1908-1989) whose astonishing gift it was to us to have provided a critical edition of Wesley's *Works,* to edit a best selling critical anthology of John Wesley, and to publish a series of seminal texts on

---

[6] These are as a matter of fact not very 'theological': the distinctives include its forms of worship, its social concerns, its universalising of the scope of the gospel and the stress on the role of the laity in Methodism.

[7] Henry Rack, *Reasonable Enthusiast,* Epworth, 1989, p. 553.

[8] We owe to them, with Raymond George, *The History of Methodism in Great Britain*, Epworth, 1964-88.

[9] Thomas Langford's two books, one authored one edited, *Practical Divinity: Theology in the Wesleyan Tradition,* Abingdon, 1983, and *Doctrine and Theology in the United Methodist Church,* Kingswood Books, 1991, are mines of information about the theological renewal in Methodism. A sense of the rich variety in the approaches of the scholars I am referring to will be gained from close study of the titles mentioned in the footnotes which follow.

Wesley's thought.[10] He had the gift of raising up disciples and it is this group (with some help from Australian, British, German and Irish Methodists) who have contributed so joyously and so passionately to the renaissance in Wesleyan theology.[11]

Other factors have also transformed our theological self-consciousness. First, the world-wide Methodist movement has benefited from a search for doctrinal identity within the largest of its constituents. For some thirty years (the whole period of its formal existence: the union of the Methodist Episcopal Church with the Evangelical United Brethren took place in 1968) the United Methodist Church in the USA, together with all its Central Conferences in Europe, Africa, Latin America and Asia, has been reviewing its Confessional commitment. As William Abraham describes this process: 'Perhaps for the first time in two centuries, Wesleyan leaders had to think very seriously about the clauses in their traditions which insisted that Methodists, contrary to their own well-worn avowals, really did have confessional commitments buried in their origins and patently visible in their constitution.'[12] A vast amount of work has been done by United Methodists to get

---

[10]   The *Works of John Wesley are* being published by Abingdon and Oxford University Press, from 1984 onwards, and a total of 36 volumes is projected; the volume entitled *John Wesley* in the 'Library of Protestant Thought' series was published by the Oxford University Press, 1970; then there are such seminal monographs as *Evangelism in the Wesleyan Spirit, Theology in the Wesleyan Spirit,* just republished in one volume as *Theology and Evangelism in the Wesleyan Spirit,* by Abingdon, 1998. and his contributions to ecumenical theology, *That the World May Believe,* Board of Missions of the Methodist Church, 1966, and *The Christian Tradition and the Unity We Seek,* Oxford University Press, 1957. Lastly there is a valuable selection of his occasional writings in *The Wesleyan Theological Heritage: Essays of Albert Outler,* edited by Thomas C. Oden and Leicester R. Longden, Zondervan, 1991.

[11]   Two tangible manifestations of this renaissance are the Oxford Institutes of Methodist Theology, held every five years, and the establishment of *The Quarterly Review* published by the United Methodist Church's Board of Higher Education.

[12]   *Waking from Doctrinal Amnesia: the Healing of Doctrine in the United Methodist Church,* Abingdon Press, 1996 p. 31.

their confessional stance made clear, and this has spilled over to other parts of the world Methodist family.

A second and significant factor has been the strong participation of the world Methodist confessional family in the work of the World Council of Churches. From its outset Methodists have offered significant leadership in all parts of the W.C.C., nowhere more so than in the Faith and Order Movement. Methodists from around the world have shared in the Faith and Order study on the Apostolic Faith, and have responded to the 1982 Lima Text on Baptism, Eucharist and Ministry (BEM).[13] The American Methodist John Deschner was for many years Moderator of the Faith and Order Commission, and the British Methodist Geoffrey Wainwright was chairman of the formative BEM sections of the Faith and Order conferences in Bangalore and Lima. There have been serious conversations on the part of the World Methodist Council and its member churches with Roman Catholics, with Anglicans, with Lutherans, with the Reformed Churches and with the Orthodox.[14] When Methodists have joined in Union Schemes, like the Church of South India and the Church of North India, or more recently in the Uniting Church of Australia, there have been serious reflections on and proposals of what the Methodist tradition has to contribute to a united church. At grassroots level the ecumenical movement has also challenged Methodists to ponder the whys and wherefores of remaining 'separated.'

---

[13]   Their responses now form part of the *corpus theologicum* of world wide Methodism. They are collected in *Churches Respond to BEM: Official responses to the "Baptism, Eucharist and Ministry" Text*, edited by Max Thurian, vols. 1-6, WCC, 1986-88.

[14]   See Geoffrey Wainwright, *Methodists in Dialog,* Kingswood, 1995 for a vivid picture of this purposeful activity, as well as for his own contributions to the mutual understanding between these separated traditions.

For all these reasons we are awakening from our doctrinal amnesia.[15] I hope that I can make a small contribution to this continuing re-invigoration. I write with two particular perspectives; that of an ecumenical theologian and that of a missiologist who is chiefly interested in the relation of the Christian faith to the other religious traditions of the world.

I have been a minister of the British Methodist church for forty years. For more than thirty of these I have worked in ecumenical situations; teaching Christian Doctrine in a United Theological College in Nigeria (with Anglicans and Presbyterians), preaching and pastoring in an Ecumenical University Chaplaincy and an Ecumenical Parish in the middle of England, working in the former British Council of Churches and teaching once again in the Cambridge Theological Federation (with Roman Catholics, Anglicans, and members of the United Reformed Church). I write now from a theological seminary which is wholly ecumenical though founded by the Christian Church (Disciples of Christ). In all these situations I have been challenged to teach or reflect upon Methodist theology, and have had to ask myself 'why am I still a Methodist?'

In the midst of all this I discovered a vocation to become a missiologist and a student/practitioner of interfaith dialogue. For thirty-five years now I have studied other religions and have interacted with their adherents. In this work I have been grateful to have inherited a theology which allows me to relate ungrudgingly to the different faith traditions. People of other Christian backgrounds often had real difficulty in being as open and as generous to truth and holiness outside the church just because of the

---

15   The phrase comes from the title of William Abraham's book already cited.

'theological entails' of their traditions. [16] Roman Catholics, Lutherans, Presbyterians, Baptists, even Anglicans were all involved in overcoming their Latinate theologies (*extra ecclesiam nulla salus, extra Christum nulla salus*) of exclusion and restriction.[17]

So I will speak with some passion and conviction of both the distinctiveness and the relevance of Methodist theology. I believe the Wesleyan pattern of theologizing ought to be seen as a 'classical theology' in its own right. But I have no intention of suggesting that it is normative, authoritative and prescriptive. In terms of its own self-understanding that would be impossible. But I do want to suggest that Methodism is a form of 'classical Christianity' and as such may justly stand alongside other forms of 'classical Christianity.' But what is 'classical Christianity'?

Classical Christianity

The expression 'Classical' bears a moment of reflection. Usage suggests three main areas of meaning. The first has to do with the ancient civilisations of Greek and Roman, especially to their art, architecture and literature. The Classical languages are Latin and Greek, no more and no less. So far there is no problem because these are matters of pure description. But quite other semantic dimensions have opened up during European history, particularly when 'Classical' came to mean that which pertained to aesthetic attitudes based upon Greek and Roman culture. Form, simplicity, proportion and restraint in emotion came

---

[16]   For the 'theological entails' of Catholicism, Lutheranism and Calvinism see Kenneth Cracknell, *Toward a New Relationship: Christians and People of Other Faith*, Epworth, 1986, pp. 9-11.

[17]   For elucidation of this somewhat cryptic comment see *my Justice, Courtesy and Love: Theologian and Missionaries Encountering World Religions, 1846-1914*. Epworth, 1995.

to be held as the highest virtues. 'Classical' was a value judgement suggesting that the Greeks and the Romans had it right. In the next extension of its range of meaning, 'Classical' denoted the highest rank or excellence, together with an implication of finality and insurpassability. Some book or other could be called the 'classic' in its field, thus suggesting that all other works of its type should be measured against its achievement. 'Classical' in this third range of meaning is synonymous with such terms as 'standard', 'normative', or 'authoritative'.

When 'classical' is used to describe Christianity, a similar range of meanings may be discerned. Thus 'Classical Christianity' may mean no more than the Christianity of the Greek and Latin Mediterranean world of the first five centuries of the Christian era. All the books known to me with 'Classical Christianity' (there are very few of them) in their titles mean exactly this.[18] 'Classical' here denotes the time period without any implication of normative or prescriptive meanings.

But in recent times another usage has crept in. Thus Thomas C. Oden refers variously to 'the classical ecumenical consensus', 'the classical consensual framework', and to the 'core of classical Christian belief'.[19] Robert A Chiles speaks of 'the central emphasis Methodism shares with Protestantism and Classical Christianity;'[20] and Geoffrey Wainwright refers to the 'classic ecumenical movement'.[21] As used by these writers, 'classical' or 'classic' begins to imply a value-judgment related to some standard achieved

---

[18]   I can find only two such in the American 'Books in Print': the Mary Couts Burnett Library of Texas Christian University (700,000 vols.) has only two titles -- the self-same ones.

[19]   Thomas C. Oden, *Doctrinal Standards in the Wesleyan Tradition*, Francis Asbury Press, 1988, pp. 99 and 310; *Agenda for Theology*, Harper and Row, 1979, p. 21.

[20]   *Op.cit.* p. 30.

[21]   *Op.cit.* p. 335.

at another time and in another context. The term 'classical' then begins to form part of an ideology of normativeness, authoritativeness and prescriptiveness. Methodist theology may be then weighed in this balance and be found wanting.

To be sure those who are not Methodists have every right to make their criticisms of our theology, and equally surely, Methodists are committed to dialogue with those who think that we have got it wrong. But in our own time we are also confronted with appeals to re-shape Methodist thinking in terms of 'classical Christianity' by Methodist themselves, occasionally in rather strident terms. Such belabouring of Methodists by fellow Methodists may be taken as one manifestation of theological disorder. Other symptoms of this disorder include a lost coherence around a universally acknowledged central theme (too much theological pluralism), a loss of satisfactory ways to explain ourselves to one another (a lack of commonly accepted discourse), and a deep dissatisfaction with Methodist preaching (in the USA at least many of the sermons I hear are based on an unbiblical psychologism and moralism). Other parts of the syndrome include the hankering after what, to Methodists, are false gods, many of which can be discerned in the nostrums and cure-alls that are often suggested as the remedy for what they see as the Methodist 'malaise'.

Such prescriptions are many and various. Five of them are worth commenting on because some of them are believed to be precisely the 'classical Christianity' from which Methodism has gone astray. They are (i) a return to Biblicism; (ii) a retreat to the positions achieved by the church in the Mediterranean world in the first five centuries of its life, (iii) a revitalization of the high theology of the Prot-

estant Reformation and great Puritan divines; (iv) the re-
establishment of a form of Wesleyan scholasticism, v)
and, this is possibly the most dangerous, even greater as-
similation to those modes of evangelical piety which first
prevailed in the nineteen and early twentieth centuries.[22]
These have become 'the old-time religion' of the mytho-
logical past ('when our chapels were full' in Britain, 'when
we had ten million members', in the USA, 'when we had
real missionaries' in some of the newer Methodist communities). Some brief comments are necessary on why
each of these solutions is frankly impossible.

(i) Perhaps the most advocated solution is a return to the
Bible. Was not Wesley a 'man of one Book'? Did he not
believe that Methodism was merely the religion of the Bible? Here the problem is not the authority of the Bible,
about which Methodists are not in dispute (as we shall see
very soon). Rather the issue is how to assess and interpret
that authority. For the Bible is neither to be trivialised nor
to be idolised. The towering grandeur of the scriptural
revelation of God is made of no account when late twentieth century people find in the Bible just the pale images of
their own prejudices. The Scriptures are used idolatrously
when texts are taken at their face value or ripped from their
contexts, and used without love and without compassion in
despite of the Biblical revelation of a God who is all love
and all compassion. Few texts have been more full of ter-
ror than Matthew 27.25, 'His blood be upon us and upon
our children.' These words and others like them have war-

---

[22]   One testimony to this shift is Frederick Dennison Maurice, writing in 1871. He
wrote: 'Immensely valuable as I hold the Methodist preaching of the last age to have
been, with the Evangelical movement in the Church and among the Dissenters which
was the result of it - utterly dead as I conceive the faith of the English nation would
have become without this rekindling of it, - I cannot but perceive that it made the sinful
man and not the God of all Grace the foundation of Christianity.' *Theological Essays,*
Macmillan, third edn, 1871, p. xvi. Maurice is both right and wrong, because, as we
shall see, although Wesley himself did his best to make the 'God of all grace' the
fountain of his theology, the succeeding generations regressed to 'sinful man.'

ranted persecutions of the Jews from Constantine through to the Holocaust. The words about 'hewers of wood and drawers of water' in Joshua 9.27 became the justification of oppression and exploitation of the Black peoples in apartheid South Africa. Terrified women were tortured and burnt in Europe and in colonial America because of Exodus 22.18: 'Thou shalt not suffer a witch to live'. Christian churches (including the Methodist Episcopal Church South) saw the institution of African slavery as founded on the basis of 'slaves be subject to your masters' (Eph. 6.5). From Augustine onwards 'Compel them to come in' (Luke 14.23) has been a mandate for forcible conversions, both of heretics and unbelievers. Paul's instructions 'to deliver this man to Satan for the destruction of the flesh, that the spirit may be saved in the day of the Lord' (1 Cor 5.5) set in motion the Inquisition and the Autos de Fé, the martyrdoms of Anabaptists in Germany, of Protestant reformers in Oxford, of Catholic recusants in London, and Quakers in the Commonwealth of Massachusetts. Paul's words, 'Let women be silent in the churches, for it is not permitted for them to speak, but to be in subjection as the law says' (1 Cor 14.34), 'the head of every man is Christ and head of the woman is the man.' (1 Cor 11.3), and that a man bears 'the image and glory of God, but the woman is the glory of the man' (1 Cor 11.7) have led to the demeaning of women throughout Christian history. Even the over-fishing of the oceans, the destruction of the rain forests and the execrable treatment of animals in factory farms have had their biblical justification: 'fill the earth and subdue it, have dominion over the fish of the sea and over the birds of the air and over every living thing' (Gen. 1.28). Maybe we could argue this avalanche of oppression and suffering has arisen through misinterpretation of Scripture (what, all of it?), but the recital of these texts (there are many others) indicates that most of us need serious hermeneutic tools in our Biblical interpretation.[23] It is not possible mindlessly to affirm with Biblical literalists, 'the Bible says it and I believe it.' or to parrot the words of a car bumper sticker in the Bible Belt, where I now live, 'God Said It -- That Settles It.' Methodists are never quite comfortable in affirming in Christian worship, as some churches do, 'This is the Word of the Lord.'[24]

(ii) Linked to the call to go 'back to the Bible' (and offered partly as a solution to these difficulties about Biblical literalism) is the argument for a return the Christianity of the first five centuries. This form of Christian faith is posited as having attained the finest and most definitive expression of all that the Bible has to teach. As such it is presented as 'Classical Christianity'. To be sure, in the neutral or descriptive sense it is the Christianity of the classical world, its languages are Latin and Greek. But those who would argue that there is a set of doctrines 'as fixed as the sun' take it as axiomatic that the Apostles' Creed, the Nicene Creed, the Athanasian Creed, and the Chalcedonian definition are accurate summaries of biblical teaching.[25] But the chief difficulty here lies with the amount of lumber that one has to take on board accurately to understand whether or not this is the case, because the historical debates which produced such formulas assume philosophical conceptions far removed from our own epistemological frameworks. Concepts like person (Latin *persona,* if this accurately represents what is meant by the Greek *hypostasis*), satisfaction (*satisfactio*), substance (*ousia*) and, somewhat later meritum (*meritum*) and transubstantiation (*transubstantia-*

---

23   Which is precisely why John Wesley felt the need to provide his people with *Explanatory Notes on the New Testament*, see below.
24   The *Draft of the Methodist Worship Book* being presented at the Scarborough Conference of the British Methodist Church, June, 1998, does not contain this formula.
25   John Wesley had some reservations about the Athanasian Creed, with its imprecations, and deleted Article VIII (Of the Three Creeds) in his selection of the *Articles of Religion* for the American Methodist Church.

tio), used freely by the Church Fathers from Tertullian onwards, have their roots in Roman Law and Greek Philosophy. To a missiologist, the linking of a 'final' statement of the faith to a cultural-linguistic episode looks like the absolutizing of an acute form of contextualization. All our missionary experience now tells us that Christ in his universal relevance will be portrayed using other metaphysical schemes and other conceptualities without passing first through the prism of Hellenistic and Roman thought.[26] There are other elements as well in the acute hellenization of Christianity which disqualify this period from being regarded as normative and prescriptive. [27]

(iii) But perhaps the great reformers like Martin Luther and John Calvin are more like us, and lived in world nearer to the one we live in. So the solution is to recover their standards, for, as we are reminded in the British Doctrinal Clause, the Methodist Church 'loyally accepts the fundamental principles' of the Protestant Reformation. The Lutheran aspect ought to be particularly congenial to Methodists because Wesley himself once wrote of Martin

---

[26]   From a vast literature on the subject, I choose just four in order to take non-missiologists into the kinds of shifts and transformations that the Christian faith must move into as it becomes at home in different cultures. David Bosch, *Transforming Mission: Paradigm Shifts in Theology of Mission*, Orbis, 1991, see especially his comments on 'the missionary paradigm of the Eastern Church' pp. 194-213; Andrew W. Walls, *The Missionary Movement in Christian History: Studies in the Transmission of Faith*, T. and T. Clark and Orbis, 1996. Note particularly his remarks on early orthodoxy as 'logically expounded belief set in codified form, and maintained through effective organisation.' He continues: 'Hellenistic Roman civilisation offered a total system of thought, and expected general conformity to its norms. The Christian penetration of the system inevitably left it a total system.' pp. 19ff. Thomas J. Thangaraj, *The Crucified Guru: an Experiment in Cross Cultural Christology*, Abingdon, 1995, and Vincent Donovan, *Christian Rediscovered: an Epistle from the Masai*, Orbis, 1978, show graphically how Christianity is not necessarily to be conformed to that 'total system.'

[27]   For example: if we compare the Nicene Creed with the Sermon on the Mount, ethical instruction has become secondary or non existent in relation to dogma, so that the Nicene Creed makes a number of doctrinal statements intelligible within its own metaphysical frame work, but says nothing whatsoever about ethics. Orthodoxy (right belief) has taken precedence over orthopraxis (right action). This would be the chief complaint of liberation theologians like Gustavo Gutièrrez and the Argentinean Methodist José Miguez Bonino.

Luther as 'a man highly favoured of God and a blessed instrument',[28] and ever since the pioneering work of George Croft Cell, *The Rediscovery of John Wesley* published as long ago as 1935,[29] Wesleyans have been rediscovering the greatness of John Calvin. Others among us think we should refresh ourselves with insights from great Puritan teachers like Richard Baxter and John Owen.[30] Let us, they appear to suggest, wrap ourselves in 'the Banner of Truth.' But here 'truth' is a highly problematic expression. It was in the name of truth that Martin Luther preached so fearsomely against 'The Jews and their Lies'[31], and in the name of truth that he justified the death penalty for Mennonites, Baptists, Schwenkfelder and other 'sects.'[32] It was equally in the name of 'truth' that John Calvin consented (if reluctantly) to the burning of Michael Servetus in Geneva and in the name of truth that Congregationalist Puritans hanged Quakers on Boston Common. Certainly Luther and Calvin and the Puritans do not have to be brought before the bar of modern liberal humanism: they were people of a different age. But this gives us every reason to question their theologies and ecclesiologies when these were developed beyond their 'fundamental principles'. This is not only because the Reformers used the sword and the stake, but because a number of conse-

---

[28]   Quoted by E. Gordon Rupp in *The Righteousness of God: Luther Studies,* Hodder and Stoughton, 1953, p. 45.

[29]   Publ. by Henry Holt Co, 1935.

[30]   A book which accurately assesses what Methodists can still learn from the Puritans is *Robert C. Monk, John Wesley: His Puritan Heritage,* Abingdon, 1966. But note Monk's quotation of Gordon Wakefield, 'The Puritan stress on the moment and process of cf. conversion and the agonised search for assurance tended to give the spiritual life a perpetual squint of self-regard. It too ruthlessly schematised the struggles of certain rare men of spiritual genius and made them a pattern for the many, 'Puritanism, its Necessity, Dangers and Future', *Methodist Sacramental Fellowship Bulletin,* Summer, 1961, p. 4, see also Gordon Wakefield, *Puritan Devotion: its Place in the Development of Christian Piety,* Epworth, 1957.

[31]   I say balefully because no less than eighteen editions of this work *Von den Jueden und Ihren Luegen* were printed in Nazi Germany.

[32]   This information, and that in the previous note, comes from Franklin H. Littell, 'United Methodism in a World of Religious Diversity', in Arvind Sharma (ed.), *Fragments of Infinity: Essays in Religion and Philosophy,* Prism, 1991, p. 128.

quences followed their single-minded commitment to proving themselves in the right. First, they cast their theologies in a polemic and combative mode. Some of their followers today appear to think that is still the only way of proceeding in theological matters. Second, they left a fearful legacy of resentment and bitterness in the hearts of the 'other side', whoever that other side was, which often lingers still as a 'non-theological factor' at the back of ecumenical dialogue. Third, and not least, a missiologist must say that their overwhelming concern with 'truth' also prevented any real concern for mission outside 'Christendom' (for us a thoroughly antiquated conception but very real to them). These people were too busy arguing with each other about claiming existing territory within 'Christendom' to have been bothered about the ends of the earth.[33] For these and other reasons, it would be unwise to take on board Reformation theology without a serious awareness of the differences between the age of Luther and Calvin and our own.[34] In any case since Methodist theology is not focussed upon 'truth', it has quite another trajectory. As Albert Outler has put it, the contrast between Wesleyan theology and Reformation theologies goes like this. Wesleyan theology, he says, is 'a theology less interested in the order of Christian *truth* (as in school theologies generally) than in the Christian *life*. Its specific focus is the order of salvation as an eventful process that stretches

---

[33] See my brief discussion of why 'mission to the ends of the earth' had to wait for another two centuries before it really gripped the imaginations of Protestant Christians in *Justice Courtesy and Love: Theologians and Missionaries Encountering World Religions, 1846-1914*, pp. 288-9. I wrote there that their most serious issue was 'Which is the true church? Descriptions of the nature of the church became self-serving and inward looking. There was little sense of any 'kingdom' beyond the four walls of the sacred places of each denomination.'

[34] For a sense of the distance that lies between Luther's concerns and those of St. Paul, and between Luther and Christians living in the last years of the twentieth century, see Krister Stendahl's remarkable essay, 'The Apostle Paul and the Introspective Conscience of the West' in *Paul among Jews and Gentiles*, Fortress Press, 1976, pp. 78-96.

across the whole horizon of Christian existence.'[35] We may add that this process also stretches far beyond the horizon of Christian existence as lived out within 'Christendom.'

(iv) 'Back to Wesley' is the slogan of many others. This is perhaps the most appropriate of all these solutions for the people called Methodists, and it is made the more attractive by the magnificent resurgence in Wesleyan studies in our own time. We have already referred to the great contemporary team of scholars which has enabled us to see the Wesleyan theological achievement in new clarity and relevance.[36] But even so a form of Wesleyan scholasticism is not a viable option.[37] Vast changes have taken place in the last two hundred years. For all his genius Wesley lacked the historical consciousness which most contemporary theology presupposes. He does not, because he could not, address those understandings of individual and social psychology upon which all contemporary pastoral theology and pastoral counselling are based. He cannot leap out of his eighteenth century skin to help us with those issues in bio-ethics and genetic engineering brought to the forefront

---

[35] 'A New Future for Wesley Studies: an Agenda for "Phase III"', in M. Douglas Meeks, *The Future of the Wesleyan Theological Traditions*, Abingdon, 1985, p. 44, emphasis his.

[36] Along with the works of Outler already cited may be put Colin W. Williams, *John Wesley's Theology for Today*, Abingdon, 1960, Lycurgus M. Starkey, *The Work of the Holy Spirit: a Study in Wesleyan Theology*, Abingdon, 1962, Mildred Bangs Wynkoop, *A Theology of Love: the Dynamic of Wesleyanism*, Beacon Hill, 1972, Robert Cushman, *John Wesley's Experimental Divinity: Studies in Methodist Doctrinal Standards*, Kingswood, 1989, Robert C. Tuttle, *Mysticism in the Wesleyan Tradition*, Francis Asbury Press, 1989, Ted Campbell, *John Wesley and Christian Antiquity*, Kingswood, 1991, Randy L. Maddox, *Responsible Grace*, Kingswood, 1994, Thomas C. Oden, *John Wesley's Scriptural Christianity: a Plain exposition of his Teaching on Christian Doctrine*, Zondervan, 1994, Scott C. Jones, *John Wesley's Conception and Use of Scripture*, Abingdon, 1995, Richard P. Heitzenrater, *Wesley and the People Called Methodist*, Abingdon, 1995. An ecumenical as well as a Wesleyan overview can be found in M. Douglas Meeks, *What Should Methodists Teach? Wesleyan Tradition and Modern Diversity*, Kingswood, 1990.

[37] John B. Cobb Jr. has set out exactly why this is so in his *Grace and Responsibility: A Wesleyan Theology for Today*, Abingdon, 1995. Some of his phraseology is reflected in the sentences which follow.

of our attention by every new advance of medical science. He has no healing word to our controversies about sexuality and gender issues.[38] He lived well before the revolution in the self-understanding of women. He could not have even considered the possible of homosexuality being a genetic rather than an acquired condition. The 'tidal wave of criticisms' (John B. Cobb's expression) of Christianity in terms of its anti-Judaism, if not its downright antisemitism; of its patriarchal modality and its long history of the oppression of women; of its Euro-centrism and apparently in-built racist tendencies, of its identification with imperialism and its ever ready support of colonialism, of its anthropocentrism and destructive 'domination' of all other species never impinged on Wesley's mind at all.[39]

(v) Yet another assumption is that all would be well again if we were to embrace afresh the pieties of the late nineteenth and early twentieth centuries, and indeed conformed more closely to those contemporary groupings which represent their survival into the late twentieth century. Five features of this 'old time religion' would make this a deleterious process. They are 1) intensely individualistic, 2) sectarianly fundamentalist 3) premillenarist, and therefore 4) extractionist in their understanding of salvation, 5) and either a-sacramental or anti-sacramental. Some of these features reflect the enlightenment period in which they were born, for example (1) the extreme individualism of this period. John Wesley himself was sensitive to this basic error of eighteenth century perceptions. As he emphasized many times, the Bible knows nothing of a solitary religion: 'Christianity is essentially a social religion ... to

---

[38] In the course of writing this little book, I have looked at his 'explanatory notes' on Paul's view of women. They are silent about the real issues. He also avoids the issue of slavery by translating *doulos* as servant.

[39] *Grace and Responsibility: A Wesleyan Theology for Today*, Abingdon, 1995, p. 7.

turn it into a solitary religion, is indeed to destroy it.'[40] To be sure he is talking of fugitive and cloistered religion which does not face the world but retreats into private experience but the point remains: he would repudiate spiritual self-seeking as the highest goal of religion. The overweening emphasis on 'me', 'my soul', and 'my salvation' which infected Catholics and Protestants alike in the nineteenth and twentieth centuries has been corrected by renewed emphases on the one hand arising from Biblical theology (the idea of 'corporate personality' in the Old Testament and of the 'body of Christ' in the New Testament) and on the other by the continuous rebuke of individualism by Christians of non-Western cultures.[41] (2) Despite its widespread contemporary usage to describe anything we dislike (Islamic fundamentalism, Hindu fundamentalism and so on) fundamentalism is properly a set of doctrines and concomitant behaviour centred upon a series of tracts called *The Fundamentals* written between 1910 and 1915, which became the rallying point for the anti-modernist movements in American Protestantism.[42] In each of these works was set out a militantly conservative position, asserting, for example, the truth of the Biblical six day creation narrative in the face of the scientific understanding of evolution. Such a back-to-the-wall mentality has no part in Methodist thinking. Some words of

---

[40] From Sermon 24, *On the Sermon on the Mount,* Fourth Discourse, Wesley continues: 'By Christianity I mean that method of worshipping God which is here revealed to man by Jesus Christ. When I say, This is essentially a social religion, I mean not only that it cannot subsist so well, but that it cannot subsist at all, without society, — without living and conversing with other men. And in showing this, I shall confine myself to those considerations which will arise from the very discourse before us. But if this be shown, then, doubtless, to turn this religion into a solitary one is to destroy it.' *Works*, Vol.1, p. 533.

[41] For further reading see the seminal chapter in David Bosch's *Transforming Mission: Paradigm Shifts in Theology of Mission,* entitled 'Mission in the Wake of the Enlightenment', pp. 262-345; and the rich variety of African perceptions recorded by Vincent Donovan in *Christianity Rediscovered.*

[42] Published by Testimony Publishing Co of Chicago, this series of twelve paperback volumes was edited by R. A. Torrey and A. C. Dixon. Financed by two Chicago laymen, they were sent to every Pastor, Missionary and Sunday School teacher that could be traced throughout the world. About three million copies were circulated.

William Abraham to describe United Methodism are apposite; he says that it identifies itself not 'as a narrow sect, holding a reduced set of doctrines, but as a church which stands in the great historical tradition ... moreover we [sc. United Methodists] clearly are not committed to even an echo of the Fundamentalist doctrine of scripture.'[43] (3) One important area for the exponents of *The Fundamentals'* was the imminent physical Return of Christ. Until happened, little could be done to alter the state of things and souls needed to be saved from the world. This teaching had grown up in the 1830s and 1840s with Edward Irving and J.N. Darby [44] and led eventually to the founding of missionary societies which sought to fulfil the text: 'The Gospel of the Kingdom shall be preached in the whole world for a testimony to all the nations, and then shall the end come' (Matt 24.14)[45] The Pentecostal movements emerging from this period (classical Pentecostalism') were stoutly pre-millennialist and have remained so. The upsurge in missionary work produced some great figures, and it is understandable that some Methodists would want to emulate both their charismatic enthusiasm and their evangelistic fervour. But Methodist theology does not sit comfortably with premillennialism. Its spirit is much more postmillennialist, concerned for the kingdom of Jesus here and now in this world. As we shall soon see, John Wesley believed that this world had to be renewed in justice and in

---

[43] *Awaking from Doctrinal Amnesia: the Healing of Doctrine in United Methodist Church.,* p.67. Nor for that matter is any strand of the tradition: the Wesleyan Holiness theologian Floyd Cunningham is very specific: that the 'fundamentalist leavening' in Holiness traditions, 'evident in the rise in premillennialism and assumptions about Biblical inerrancy' are not 'inherently part of the tradition'. 'Interreligious Dialogue: a Wesleyan Holiness Perspective', in S. Mark Heim (ed.), *Grounds for Understanding: Ecumenical Resources for Responses to Religious Pluralism,* Eerdmans, 1998, p.189.

[44] The former was the founder of the Catholic Apostolic Church, and one of the original source of Pentecostalism, the second name the founder of the Plymouth Brethren and ultimate begetter of the Schofield Reference Bible in which 'Dispensationalism' is laid out.

[45] Among these were the Regions Beyond Missionary Union, founded in 1878; the Christian and Missionary Alliance, founded in 1887; and the Evangelical Alliance Mission founded in 1890.

peace. Charles Wesley taught Methodists to sing of the time of Jubilee[46] and the time when warfare and fighting should cease. In common with Jonathan Edwards, Isaac Watts, George Frederick Handel, William Blake, and the founders of the mainstream missionary societies, both Wesleys were postmillennialists.[47] (4) Hand in hand with premillennialism though goes an otherworldly or 'extractionist' understanding of salvation. To be saved is to taken out of this world, and one mark of this is separation from the world. The idea of the conventicle as the exclusive community of the godly is also intrinsic to this conception. Again all Wesleyan theology tends in the other direction

> Freely to all ourselves we give
> Constrain'd by Jesu's love to live
> The servants of mankind.[48]

(5) Last, but not least, among the dangers of aligning ourselves with those forms of Protestantism which emerged in the last one hundred and fifty years is their widespread misunderstanding of the nature of sacramentalism. The central issue here is whether sacraments are humanly devised forms of ritual and ceremony which are either dependent and consequent upon human profession of faith, or whether God is both the author and the chief agent in sacramental activity, using the physical material of the divine creation to work spiritual marvels. The Methodist

---

[46] 'Blow ye the trumpet, blow/ The gladly solemn sound. / Let all the nations know/ To earth's remotest bound; /The Year of Jubilee is come! / return, ye ransomed sinners, home', a hymn which was very well known in the USA (it is No. 379 in the United Methodist Hymnal), where postmillennnialism was part of the founding myth of the nation, and 'Come, Saviour, from above/ O'er all our hearts to reign/ and plant the kingdom of thy love /In every heart of man/ then fightings and wars shall cease/ And, in thy Spirit given/ Pure joy and everlasting peace/ shall turn our earth to heaven.' *Collection of Hymns for the Use of People called Methodists* No. 435, *Works*, 7:612.

[47] The U.S journal *The Prophetic Times* specifically condemned 'the expectation of a Millennium of universal righteousness and peace before the return of the Savior' as an 'unchristian delusion'; the postmillennialism as a the earliest missionary motive see my *Justice Courtesy and Love; Theologians and Missionaries Encountering World Religions, 1846-1914*, pp 4-11.

[48] *Collection of Hymns for the Use of People Called Methodists* (1878 edn), No.526.

churches in both the British and the American tradition adhere to the words set out in Article 16 of the American doctrinal standards: sacraments are 'not only badges or tokens' but also 'certain signs of grace and God's good will to us'.[49] To be sure many sections of the growing Methodist movement in the nineteenth century neglected to administer either sacrament. As Thomas Frank describes it in what he calls the 'unstructured context of America

> Methodist preachers felt complete freedom to ignore Wesley's Anglican liturgy for Sunday Service, and to neglect the Lord's Supper as of secondary status. After all had not Wesley himself argued that preaching was absolutely central for bringing people to salvation, and the Lord's Supper but one of the means of grace? The circuit riders organised societies, not congregations, and encouraged the people to build chapels not churches. The preachers itinerated constantly; they were decidedly not resident priests providing pastoral services to a parish. [50]

Parallels could be drawn with the development of British Methodism and particularly in those segments which separated from the main tradition. The greatest example of this would be the Salvation Army.[51] But eventually the societies did turn into congregations, and the chapels into churches, and there was a need to restore the full range of pastoral services to Methodist people. The living Wesleyan tradition has had once more to reveal its treasures and on both sides of the Atlantic, indeed throughout world

---

[49]   This is No. XXV of the *Articles of Religion* of the Church of England. and No. XVI of the *Articles of Religion* of the Methodist Church.

[50]   Thomas Edward Frank, *Polity, Practice and the Mission of the United Methodist Church*, Abingdon, 1997, p. 58.

[51]   'The Salvation Army is uniquely non sacramentarian in its religious life. The Army is not anti-sacramental; rather, it believes that grace is mediated in direct communion with Christ and the Holy Spirit, rather than by church rites and ordinances. In worship the Salvationist often sings what some call the sacramental song of the Army, composed by the poet General (1946-54), Albert Osborn: 'My life must be Christ's broken bread,/ My love his outpoured wine.' Henry Gariepy, *Christianity in Action, The Salvation Army in the USA Today*, Victor Books, 1990, pp. 25-6.

Methodism, a rediscovery of the sacramental traditions has been taking place.[52] A community of faith which has among those treasures these words will not go wholly astray.

> Come Father, Son and Holy Ghost;
> Honour the means ordained by thee;
> Make good our apostolic boast
> And own thy glorious ministry.
>
> We now thy promised presence claim;
> Sent to disciple all mankind,
> Sent to baptize into thy name,
> We now thy promised presence find
>
> Father, in these reveal thy Son,
> In these, for whom seek thy face,
> The hidden mystery make known,
> The inward, pure, baptising grace.
>
> Jesus, with us thou always art;
> Effectuate now the sacred sign.
> The gift unspeakable impart,
> And bless the ordinance divine.
>
> Eternal spirit descend from high,
> Baptizer of our spirits thou!
> The sacramental seal apply
> And witness with the water now!
>
> O that the souls baptized therein
> May now thy truth and mercy feel;
> May rise, and wash away their sin!
> Come, Holy Ghost, their pardon seal! [53]

---

[52] In Britain the Methodist Sacramental Fellowship and in the USA the Order of St. Luke have exerted an influence on the renewal of Methodist worshipping life out of all proportion to the size of their memberships. We may take it that they have been ministering to long-felt needs among Methodist people.

[53] *Hymns for the Use of the People Called Methodists*, 1780, No. 464, *Works*, Vol 7, p. 646; *Hymns and Psalms*, No 580 Interestingly, since this hymn is based on the 'Great Commission', Matt. 28.18-20, Geoffrey Wainwright makes its the staring point for his brief sketch of a Methodist theology of mission, see Dean S. Galliland, *The World Forever Our Parish*, Bristol Books, 1991, pp. 157-69.

Twice Charles Wesley insists on the sacrament of baptism as divine ordinance: 'the means ordained by thee' and 'the ordinance divine'. He asserts the work of Christ within the 'mystery' in the washing away of sins. Note also that for him it was 'Spirit baptism': 'come Holy Ghost, their pardon seal'. Concerning the Eucharist, or the Lord's Supper, he wrote:

> Jesus, we thus obey
> Thy last and kindest word;
> Herein thy own appointed way'
> We come to meet thee, Lord
>
> Our heart we open wide
> To make the Saviour room,
> And lo! The Lamb the crucified,
> The sinners' friend is come.
>
> His presence makes the feast;
> And now our spirits feel,
> The glory not to be expressed,
> The joy unspeakable.
> ....
>
> He bids us drink and eat
> Imperishable food;
> He gives his flesh to be our meat,
> And bids us drink his blood.
>
> Whate'er the Almighty can
> To pardoned sinners give,
> The fullness of our God made man.
> We here with Christ receive.[54]

A Church which sings this has not lost the great tradition of the Christian faith. In the obedience to dominical command ('We thus obey'), in the claiming of the 'real presence' ('his presence makes the feast'), the use of the two elements (bread and wine: 'his flesh ... his blood'), and

---

54 *Hymns and Psalms*, No. 614.

sense of the reception of the 'fulness of our God made man' are true marks of Catholicity.

Chapter Two

The Methodist Movement's Theology.

1. 'It ever remembers'

The most striking formulation of the Doctrinal Clause of the Deed of Union of the British Methodist Churches in 1932 says that it 'ever remembers that in the Providence of God Methodism was raised up to spread Scriptural Holiness throughout the land ...' To make such a statement is evidence of a certain kind of self-awareness. Methodist identify themselves by 'remembering'. Such a self-description makes British Methodism different in kind from forms of magisterial Protestantism, whether Congregationalist, Presbyterian, Baptist, or Evangelical Anglicanism. These great sister denominations base their existence, their theology, and their church order upon distinctive understandings of the New Testament. None of these Churches requires any sense of a special vocation to assure its legitimacy: each one views itself as merely in continuity with the New Testament church, whether by tradition or by rediscovery. From a Methodist point of view their readings of the New Testament usually appear self-justifying and tendentious.

The dominant theme of this corporate memory is that they were 'raised up to spread scriptural holiness throughout the land'. [55] Consequently Methodists begin doing theology

---

[55]   The American version runs likes this: 'Q.4 What may we reasonably believe to be God's design in raising up the Preachers called Methodists? A. To reform the continent, and to spread scriptural Holiness over these Lands' *Minutes of Several*

by telling their version of the Wesleyan revival of religion in the Eighteenth Century. This narrative makes them a distinctive community, giving them a sense of identity as 'people'. That this procedure has been in place from the beginning is clear from John Wesley's frequent recitals of this story. Here is an example from his Sermon *On the General Spread of the Gospel.*

> Let us observe what God has done already. Between fifty and sixty years ago, God raised up a few young men, in the University of Oxford, to testify those grand truths, which were then little attended to: — That without holiness no man shall see the Lord; — that this holiness is the work of God, who worketh in us both to will and to do; — that he doeth it of his own good pleasure, merely for the merits of Christ; — that this holiness is the mind that was in Christ; enabling us to walk as he also walked; — that no man can be thus sanctified till he be justified; — and, that we are justified by faith alone. These great truths they declared on all occasions, in private and in public; having no design but to promote the glory of God, and no desire but to save souls from death.
>
> From Oxford, where it first appeared, the little leaven spread wider and wider. More and more saw the truth as it is in Jesus, and received it in the love thereof. More and more found "redemption through the blood of Jesus, even the forgiveness of sins." They were born again of his Spirit, and filled with righteousness, and peace, and joy in the Holy Ghost. It afterwards spread to every part of the land, and a little one became a thousand. It then spread into North Britain and Ireland; and a few years after into New York, Pennsylvania, and many other provinces in America, even as high as Newfoundland and Nova Scotia. So that, although at first this "grain of mustard seed" was "the least of all the seeds;" yet, in

---

Conversations between the Rev. Thomas Coke, LL.D., the Rev. Francis Asbury and Others ... in the Year 1784. Composing a Form of Discipline...', p.4.

a few years, it grew into a "large tree, and put forth great branches." [56]

At any time when his revival was called into question Wesley produced this kind of evidence. We may call it his 'narrative defence': 'Let us consider what God has done...' Even his *Journal* represents the telling of the story as is plain from one slogan-text: "If this counsel or this work be of men, it will come to naught: but if it be of God ye cannot overthrow it; lest haply ye be found to fight against God" Acts 5.38,9.

There are many other evidences of this narrative mode of doing theology. The *Minutes* of his earliest Conferences were so organised as to include the 'Conversation on the Work of God.' Such conversation became a recital of the events of the previous year. This pattern was followed in North America where the *Doctrines and Disciplines* had an introductory section called: 'of the Rise of Methodism both in Europe and in America'.[57] In due course this section developed into a separate historical preface, remaining unchanged until the union of the divided Methodist Episcopal churches in 1939. Today the current United Methodist *Discipline* carries a 'Historical Preface', ensuring that all streams of the modern United Methodist Church are made aware of how they have converged, having sprung from the same source.

---

[56]   Sermon 63, *The General Spread of the Gospel, Works* , Vol. 2, p 491.

[57]   The first words of *The 'Methodist Discipline' of 1798*, are 'Dearly beloved brethren, we think it expedient to give you an account of the rise of Methodism both in Europe and America. "In 1729, two young men in England, reading the Bible saw that they could not be saved without holiness, followed after it and incited others so to do In 1737 they likewise that men are justified before they are sanctified: But still holiness was their object. God then thrust them out to raise a holy people."' Academy Books, facsimile edition 1979, p. iii.

But the most obvious example of doing theology by narrative has to do with time and space. Indeed, Wesleyanism fits well into the category of religious communities who celebrate 'sacred time' and 'sacred space'. Despite having no saint's day in the Church's calendar devoted to their founders, Methodists have a particular event to commemorate, that of May 24th, 1738:

> In the evening I went very unwillingly to a society in Aldersgate Street, where one was reading Luther's preface to the Epistle to the Romans. About a quarter before nine, while he was describing the change which God works in the heart through faith in Christ, I felt my heart strangely warmed. I felt I did trust in Christ, Christ alone for salvation: And an assurance was given me, that he had taken away my sins, even mine, and saved me from the law of sin and death.[58]

For many Methodists this narrative has been highlighted as the moment of the birth of Methodism. Each year either the evening of May 24th or the following Sunday has become 'sacred time.' What is being commemorated is the moment, as it appears, when Wesley passed from faithlessness to full assurance, from despondency to confidence, from a cold and formal religion to the religion of the heart. I say 'appears' because there is some justification for questioning Aldersgate and May 24th as the time and place of Wesley's conversion. There are two reasons for this hesitation: first, because Wesley was by any standards a devoted Christian long before 1738, and second, because Wesley himself makes so little of this experience in the following fifty years of his life.[59] It is noticeable,

---

[58] *Journal, Works,* Vol.18, pp. 249-50.

[59] See e.g. Theodore W. Jennings' *tour de force* in the *Quarterly Review,* Vol.8, No.2, Fall 1988, in which he protests against 'Aldersgatism.' Jennings writes: The dishonesty shown by those who ignore Wesley's own description of his experiences in order to claim that Wesley was converted at Aldersgate cannot be ascribed to Wesley himself. Only with time, experience and maturity would Wesley find the categories

for example, that Wesley stresses his commitment to holiness in 1725 rather than his 'Aldersgate experience' in the Sermon have just quoted.

Yet Methodists are not mistaken in believing this was a period of transformation both for Charles and John. Without a similar experience on May 21st, Charles Wesley could not have written:

> Where shall my wond'ring soul begin?
> How shall I all to heav'n aspire?
> A slave redeemed from death and sin,
> A Brand plucked from eternal fire,
> How shall I equal triumphs raise.
> Or sing my great deliverer's praise?

pledging a total commitment to telling the good news to the totally lost:

> Outcasts of men, to you I call
> Harlots, and publicans, and thieves!
> His spreads his arms to embrace you all;
> Sinners alone his grace receives;
> No need of him the righteous have;
> He comes the lost to seek and save.[60]

Only with what happened earlier in the evening of May 24th, 1738, could John Wesley have joined so gladly in singing these words at Charles Wesley's lodging. As Charles described this: 'Towards ten, my brother was brought in triumph by a troop of our friends, and declared, "I believe". We sang the hymn with great joy, and parted

---

which would make sense of incomplete faith and the progress of growing in grace, pp. 16-19. We may agree with Jennings that 'Aldersgatism' will be a pious fraud if we allow 'an experience of faith' to take the place of 'the search for holiness'. See a whole volume dedicated to these questions, Randy L. Maddox (ed.), *Aldersgate Reconsidered*, Kingswood, 1990.

60 *A Collection of Hymns for the Use of the People Called Methodists*, 1780, No 29, Works, Vol 7, p. 646; *Hymns and Psalms*, No 706

with prayer.'[61] Only with such an experience behind both of them does the 'Wesley's Birthday Hymn' make sense (It was composed by Charles Wesley of course, but made his own by John by its inclusion in the *Collection of Hymns for the Use of the People Called Methodists*):

> Away with our fears!
> The glad morning appears
> When an heir of salvation was born!
> From Jehovah I came,
> For his glory I am,
> And to him with singing I return.
>
> I sing of thy grace
> From my earliest days.
> Ever near to allure and defend;
> Hitherto thou hast been
> My preserver from sin,
> And I trust thou wilt save to the end.
> ....
>
> What a mercy is this,
> What a heaven of bliss,
> How unspeakably happy am I;
> Gathered into thy fold,
> With thy people enrolled.
> With thy people to live and to die.
> ....
>
> In a rapture of joy
> My life I employ
> The God of my life to proclaim;
> 'Tis worth living for this,
> To administer bliss,
> And salvation in Jesus's name.
>
> My remnant of days,
> I spend in his praise,
> Who died the whole world to redeem;
> Be they many of few,

---

61   Charles Wesley, *Journal*, quoted from Arnold Dillmore, *A Heart Set Free: the Life of Charles Wesley*, Crossway Books, 1988, pp.62-3

My days are his due,
And they all are devoted to him.[62]

Without the events of May, 1738, Jonathan Edwards' account of the revival of religion in Northampton in New England would not have made such a great an impact on John Wesley. So great was this impression that the Great Awakening would become his model for his own mission and Jonathan Edwards' interpretation of it his own theology of 'the religious affections.' In John Wesley's words:

> On Monday, 9, I set out for Oxford. In walking I read the truly surprising narrative of the conversions lately wrought in and about the town of North Hampton, in New-England. Surely "this is the Lord's doing, and it is marvellous in our eyes."[63]

Without the events of May, 1738, Wesley would not have consented in the following Spring 'to become more vile,' and so to begin his life's work of open air preaching. On March 29th he says:

> I left London, and in the evening expounded to a small company at Basingstoke. Saturday, 31. In the evening I reached Bristol, and met Mr. Whitefield there. I could scarce reconcile myself at first to this strange way of reaching in the fields, of which he set me an example on Sunday; having been all my life (till very lately) so tenacious of every point relating to decency and order, that I should have thought the saving of souls almost a sin, if it had not been done in a church.

---

[62]   *A Collection of Hymns for the Use of the People Called Methodists,* 1780, No 221, *Works,* Vol 7, p. 357; *Hymns and Psalms ,* No. 664. Charles seems to have composed this hymn on his birthday, December 18th 1741.

[63]   Actually: *A Faithful Narrative of the Surprising Work of God in the Conversion of Many Hundred Souls in Northampton in New England. In a Letter to the rev. Dr. Benjamin Coleman of Boston* ...(1737). Later Wesley was to republish this and other works of Jonathan Edwards, with, as Albert Outler says, the 'Calvinism carefully filtered out.' Among these works was *An Extract from a Treatise concerning the Religious Affections* in 1773.

APRIL 1. — In the evening (Mr. Whitefield being gone) I begun expounding our Lord's Sermon on the Mount, (one pretty remarkable precedent of field-preaching, though I suppose there were churches at that time also,) to a little society which was accustomed to meet once or twice a week in Nicholas-Street.

Mon. 2. — At four in the afternoon, I submitted to be more vile, and proclaimed in the highways the glad tidings of salvation, speaking from a little eminence in a ground adjoining to the city, to about three thousand people. The scripture on which I spoke was this, (is it possible any one should be ignorant, that it is fulfilled in every true Minister of Christ?) "The Spirit of the Lord is upon me, because he hath anointed me to preach the Gospel to the poor. He hath sent me to heal the brokenhearted; to preach deliverance to the captives, and recovery of sight to the blind: To set at liberty them that are bruised, to proclaim the acceptable year of the Lord."[64]

We can also add that if the times and seasons are important, so are the places of Wesley's life and ministry, particularly his birthplace in Epworth, Lincolnshire, the Chapel in City Road, and the early meeting houses of his Connexion. They have become places of pilgrimage for Methodists from around the world.

2. It has confessional standards

If story telling is where we begin doing theology, it is by no means the end. As his movement grew Wesley became concerned that the people called Methodists should have adequate doctrinal material in their hand. Accordingly his

---

[64] *Journal, ad. loc.* Note Wesley's deliberate choice of his text: it represents his abiding passion for justice for the poor and an early anticipation of the 'bias to the poor' theme of recent liberation theologies. Important studies are Theodore W. Jennings, JR., *Good News to the Poor: John Wesley's Evangelical Economics,* Kingswood, 1990, Theodore Runyon, *Sanctification and Liberation: Liberation Theologies in the Light of the Wesleyan Tradition* Abingdon, 1991, and Manfred Marquardt, *John Wesley's Social Ethics: Praxis and Principles,* Abingdon, 1992.

Sermons on Several Occasions, dating between 1746 and 1760, were his first attempt to set out the teachings which, he declared, 'I embrace and teach as the essentials of true religion'. These doctrines can be classified under five headings: 'Salvation by Faith'; 'The Assurance brought about by Faith', 'the Fruits of Faith -- Christian Behaviour'; 'Special Teaching about Christian Perfection' and 'Special Topics'.[65] They were published as the first four volumes of what was later (in 1787-8) to become an eight volume collection also known as *Sermons on Several Occasions.* In the Wesleyan Model Deed of 1763 they were designated 'the first four volumes of sermons', and later, in British Methodism, (with the addition of Sermon 35 on 'Wandering Thoughts') as *The Forty Four Sermons,* and in the USA, as *Sermons on Several Occasions* (though in America the number received as 'Standard' is 53 rather than 44), they make up, together with the *Explanatory Notes on the New Testament,* the Standards for Methodist doctrine. Wesley's opening words from the Preface to the 1746 edition make his intention clear:

> The following Sermons contain the substance of what I have been preaching for between eight and nine years last past. During that time I have frequently spoken in public, on every subject in the ensuing collection; and I am not conscious that there is any one point of doctrine, on which I am accustomed to speak in public which is not here, incidentally, if not professedly, laid before every Christian reader. Every serious man who peruses these will therefore see, in the clearest manner what those doctrines are which I embrace and teach as the essentials of true religion.

---

65   For a brief study and helpful summary of the *Sermons,* see Thomas C. Oden, *Doctrinal Standards in the Wesleyan Tradition,* Francis Asbury Press, 1988, pp. 89-99.

His *Explanatory Notes upon the New Testament* were equally as much produced as a deliberate contribution to fixing the theology of the Methodist Revival.[66] From late 1754 through to early Spring 1755 John Wesley was extremely unwell. Whatever his illness was, it made him think that his life was drawing to a close. The Preface to the *Explanatory Notes* speaks of his day being 'far spent', and that therefore, he could 'not delay any longer' in producing his exposition of the New Testament. 'Being prevented,' as he said, 'by my present weakness from either travelling or preaching,' he was still able 'to read and write, and think.' With the assistance of Johann Albrecht Bengel's *Gnomon Novi Testamenti (1742)*, Philip Doddridges's *Family Expositor,* and other writers (he acknowledges his indebtedness to them in the Preface), and with not a little help from brother Charles, Wesley set out his own version of the New Testament message, concluding that:

> In the language of the sacred writings we may observe the utmost depth, together with the utmost ease. All the elegencies of human composition sink into nothing before it: God speaks not as man, but as GOD. His thoughts are very deep; and thence his words are of inexhaustible virtue. And the language of his messengers, also, is exact in the highest degree: for the words which were given them accurately answered the impressions made upon their minds: and hence Luther says, "Divinity is nothing but a grammar of the language of the Holy Ghost."
> [67]

The importance of this 'grammar of the language of the Holy Ghost' is indicated by Wesley's own close attention

---

[66]   John Lawson comments: 'In his *Notes* the essential purpose of Wesley is to overturn the exegesis of the customary Calvinist and Antinomian proof texts, as well as to emphasise the importance of other passages in the face of formalist neglect.' *Selections from John Wesley's Notes on the New Testament: Systematically Arranged with Explanatory Comments*, Epworth, 1955, p. 10.

[67]   Preface to the *Explanatory Notes on the New Testament*, Epworth Press, many editions, p.9.

to the text, and his readiness to amend the King James Version whenever he felt it necessary, some 12,000 times in all. As a former lecturer in Greek at Oxford University, Wesley was aware of better textual methods and had access to better texts than the 1611 translators. As Thomas Oden has written, 'This is one of the most surprising aspects of the Wesleyan Doctrinal Standards -- they included, not excluded, the best available resources of critical Scripture study. Critical scholarship as not defensively avoided or grudgingly tolerated, but happily and enthusiastically undertaken as part of faith's historical honesty'.[68] The long tradition of accurate and detailed New Testament exegesis by Methodist scholars begins with John Wesley.

In 1763, John Wesley, now long since recovered from sickness and faced with the necessity to hold property in the name of his movement, produced his Model Deed for Methodist chapels and other buildings. This stipulated that trustees were responsible for ensuring that preachers in those chapel preached 'no other doctrines than is contained in Mr. Wesley's Notes upon the New Testament and four Volumes of Sermons.' It was right for the uniting Methodist Church of Great Britain in 1932 to revise its Model Deed in this spirit. Its doctrinal clause makes these grand affirmations:

> The Methodist Church claims and cherishes its place in the Holy Catholic Church, which is the Body of Christ. It rejoices in the inheritance of the Apostolic Faith and loyally accepts the fundamental principles of the historic creeds and the Protestant Reformation. It ever remembers that in the Providence of God Methodism was raised up to spread Scriptural Holiness throughout the land by the proclamation of

---

[68] *Op.cit.* p. 83.

the Evangelical Faith and declares its unfaltering re-
solve to be true to its divinely appointed mission.

3. It sings its faith

But Wesleyan theology is never merely an exposition of
John Wesley's sermons and expository notes on the
Scriptures. Our inheritance includes the great doxologies
and lyrical outbursts that make up a large proportion of
Charles Wesley's writing.[69] Albert Outler calls this phenomenon: 'the theology of John in the hymns of Charles.'[70] John Wesley would have agreed with this
judgement, once remarking that if one wanted to know his
doctrine of the Trinity it was necessary to sing his brother's
hymns.[71] But he himself could sometimes write better
theology in verse than in his prose. For example although
On the Trinity is not perhaps one of the best of his sermons, what he really felt and believed is to be found in the
hymn 'Eternal Son, Eternal Love' which concludes with
the great Trinitarian doxology:

> Blessing and honour, praise and love,
> Co-equal co-eternal Three,
> In earth below, and heaven above,
> By all thy works be paid to Thee.[72]

Echoing the ancient 'Holy, Holy, Holy' of Isaiah 6 and
the early liturgies, Charles Wesley invited the Methodist
people to sing
> Hail, holy, holy, holy Lord!
> Whom One in Three we know.

---

[69] See for the relationship of doxology and theology in our hymns, Teresa Berger, *Theology in Hymns? A Study of the Relationship of Doxology and Theology According to A Collection of Hymns for the Use of the People Called Methodists*, (1780), Kingswood, 1995.

[70] Albert Outler, *John Wesley*, p.18.

[71] John Lawson, *The Wesley Hymns: As a Guide to Scriptural Teaching*, Francis Asbury Press, 1987 is a thorough treatment of the Biblical theology of the hymnody.

[72] *Hymns and Psalms* 766.

By all the heavenly host adored,
By all thy Church below.

One undivided Trinity'
With triumph we proclaim.
The universe is full of thee,
And speaks thy glorious name.

Thee, holy Father, we confess,
Thee, holy Son, adore,
Thee, Spirit of truth and holiness,
We worship evermore.

...

Three Persons equally divine
We magnify and love,
And both the choirs ere long shall join
To sing thy praise above

Hail, Holy, holy, holy Lord.
(Our heavenly song shall be)
Supreme, essential One, adored
In co-eternal Three. [73]

There is no anti-intellectualism here. Charles Wesley neither patronises his audience nor panders to the lowest tastes or the meanest understandings. Today the presence of hymns by either of the Wesley brothers in a Methodist service guarantees adherence to that tradition of faith represented by the Apostolic and the Nicene creeds. Congregations that sing such words are indeed affirming a 'classical Christianity.' There is of course a disadvantage to using hymns as credal statements to 'sing our faith'. Not all hymn writers are as skilled theologians as the Wesley brothers. If hymns by infinitely lesser writers, who appear to be more conformed to current musical fashions, are substituted for the hymns of the great tradition, then the faith of which many Methodist congregations sing may

---

[73] *A Collection of Hymns for the Use of the People Called Methodists*, 1780, No 392, *Works*, Vol 7, p. 357; *Hymns and Psalms* No. 4.

well be far from orthodox, shifting and sliding into heretical Christology (wrong theology) and latent Calvinism (wrong ecclesiology). I fear that this is now often the case. Yet this not all that must be said about Methodist hymnody as the vehicle of our doctrinal standards. The greatest of the hymns are about the Wesleyan sense of holiness, of 'grace expressed to its ultimate conclusion' and 'transformation pushed to its utmost limits'.[74] It is particularly in them that the affective content and tone that moulds Methodist spirituality is to be experienced.

> Love divine, all loves excelling,
> Joy of heaven, to earth come down,
> Fix in us thy humble dwelling,
> All thy faithful mercies crown!
> Jesu, thou art all compassion,
> Pure, unbounded love thou art;
> Visit us with thy salvation!
> Enter every trembling heart.
>
> Come, almighty to deliver.
> Let us all thy grace receive;
> Suddenly return, and never,
> Never more thy temples leave.
> Thee we would be always blessing,
> Serve thee as thy hosts above,
> Pray and praise thee without ceasing,
> Glory in thy perfect love.
>
> Finish then thy new creation,
> Pure and spotless let us be;
> Let us see thy great salvation
> Perfectly restored in thee;
> Changed from glory into glory,
> Till in heaven we take our place,
> Till we cast our crowns before thee,
> Lost in wonder love and praise.[75]

---

[74] The phraseology is derived from H. Maldwyn Hughes, *Christian Foundations*, Epworth, 1927, pp. 162-4.
[75] *A Collection of Hymns for the Use of the People Called Methodists*, 1780, No 374, *Works*, Vol 7, p. 545.

This must be the most widely sung of all Wesleyan hymns, despite the complicated nature of the doctrine which underlies it. Much rather it is the emotional or 'affective' appeal of the words of this hymn which has given it great popularity (especially in the United Kingdom at weddings). As such, it is abiding proof that in the end of the day even the doctrine of perfect love is not itself 'the religion of the heart'.

4. Religion of the heart

From time to time John Wesley would discourse at some length on the unimportance of opinions. Sometimes he was so unguarded in this expressions that some have drawn the conclusion that it does not matter what Methodists believe. 'It is certain that opinion is not religion,' he wrote, 'no, not right opinion; assent to one, or ten thousand truths.'[76] Making this distinction between doctrinal orthodoxy (beliefs) and trust in and experience of the living God, he continues

> There is a wide difference between them: even right opinion is as distant from religion as the east is from the west. Persons may be quite right in their opinions, and yet have no religion at all; and on the other hand persons may be truly religious who hold many wrong opinions. Can anyone possibly doubt of this while there are Romanists in the world. For who can deny, not only that many of them formerly have been truly religious, as Thomas a Kempis, Gregory Lopez, and the Marquis de Renty; but that many of them even at this day, are real inward Christians? And yet what a heap of erroneous opinions do they hold, inherited from their fathers! Nay, who can doubt of it while there are Calvinists in the world.,-- asserters of absolute predestination? For who will dare to affirm that none of these are truly religious men? Not only were many of them in the last cen-

---

[76] *Sermon 55, On the Trinity, Works*, Vol. 2, pp. 374-5.

tury burning and shining lights, but many of them now are real Christians, loving God and loving all mankind. And yet what are all the absurd opinions of all the Romanists in the world, compared to that one, that the God of love, the wise, just, merciful Father of the spirits of all flesh, has from all eternity, fixed an absolute, unchangeable, irresistible decree, that part of mankind shall be saved, do what they will; and the rest, damned, do what they can.

Hence we cannot but infer, that there are ten thousand mistakes which may consist with real religion; with regard to which every candid man will think and let think. But there are some truths which are more important than others. It seems there are some which are of deep importance. I do not term them *fundamental* truths; because that is an ambiguous word; and hence there have been so many warm disputes about the number of *fundamentals*. But surely there are some which it nearly concerns us to know, as having a close connexion with vital religion. And doubtless we may rank among these that contained in the words above cited [this is the text of his Sermon]: *"There are three that bear record in heaven, the Father, the Word, and the Holy Ghost: and these three are one."* [77]

These words set the tone for the Methodist view of theology. We believe that the ability to construct infallible doctrinal formulations does not belong to the human condition. As Wesley wrote in another place:

Although every man necessarily believes that every particular opinion which he holds is true (for to believe any opinion is not true is same thing as not to hold it) yet can no man be assured that all his own opinions taken together are true. Nay, every thinking man is assured that they are not, seeing *humanum est errare et nescire* -- to be ignorant of many things. and to be mistaken in some is the necessary condition of humanity. This therefore, he is sensi-

---

[77]   *Ibid .*

ble, is his own case. He knows in general he is mistaken; though in what particulars he mistakes he does not, perhaps cannot know.[78]

Therefore we do not demand formal intellectual assent to any systematic expression of theology, a point made on both sides of the Atlantic. Doctrines remain ultimately human endeavours to express the truth about God. Formal and speculative systems are as apples to oranges when the real questions about faith or 'heart-religion' are asked. Preaching in Scotland as an old man Wesley spoke on 'Faith and Hope and Love, these three,' and then added

> A short account of Methodism, particularly insisting on the circumstances, — There is no other religious society under heaven which requires nothing of men in order to their admission in to it, but a desire to save their souls. Look all round you, you can not be admitted into the Church, or society of the Presbyterians, Anabaptists, Quakers, or any others, unless you hold the same opinions with them, and adhere to the same mode of worship. The Methodists alone do not insist on your holding this or that opinion; but they think and let think. Neither do they impose any particular mode of worship; but you may continue to worship in your former manner, be it what it may. Now, I do not know any other religious society, either ancient or modern, wherein such liberty of conscience is now allowed, or has been allowed, since the age of the Apostles. Here is our glorying; and a glorying peculiar to us. What society shares it with us?[79]

Even so, it remains an urgent priority for us all to come to right opinions. Orthodoxy, right understanding, becomes important when it directly bears upon the lived faith of the Christian. False opinions about the nature of God have led, do, and will lead to spiritual disaster. Indifference to all

---

[78] *Sermon 39, Catholic Spirit, Works*, Vol 2, pp. 83-4.
[79] *Journal*, May 18, 1788, *ad. loc.*

opinions is the 'spawn of hell, not the offspring of heaven,' for this precise reason. The need to hold the right opinions therefore leads to renewed commitment to the great themes of the Christian message. These are the truths about the very nature of God (which is formulated in the Trinitarian doctrine), and, next to these, the 'great truths of our Redemption', the ways of God's action in the world in Christ and through the power of the Spirit.[80] To these 'great truths' we now turn.

---

[80] American readers will perhaps be wondering why I have nothing here about the so-called Wesleyan Quadrilateral of Scripture, Tradition, Experience and Reason. It is simply because I do not think such a quadrilateral exists. Reason is not one equal element with the other three (all three are of necessity to be handled rationally, as best as we can, and experience does not mean the general experience of humankind, not even in the specialised empirical sense that John Locke used it, and which was sometimes espoused by John Wesley, see Richard E. Brantley, *Locke, Wesley and the Method of English Romanticism*, University of Florida Press, 1984. In the lapidary sentence of Robert E. Chiles, 'In Wesley, clarity is served by regularly reading "experience" as "evangelical experience.", *op.cit.* p. 80 .

Chapter Three
Evangelical Arminianism and Salvation Optimism

1. The Meaning of Salvation

One of the most interesting themes in Wesleyan theology is its understanding of what is meant by 'salvation'. For many parts of the Reformation tradition salvation means being forgiven, being pardoned, being justified, resulting in being made an heir of eternal life or assigned a place in heaven. But Wesley extended the semantic fields of the word 'salvation'. Two key passages give an accurate sense of John Wesley's defining terms for salvation:

> What is *salvation*? The salvation which is here spoken of is not what is frequently understood by that word, the going to heaven, eternal happiness ... it is not a blessing which lies on the other side of death, or (as we usually speak) in the other world. ... It is a present thing, a blessing which, through the free mercy of God, ye are now in possession of.[81]

> By salvation I mean, not barely, according to the vulgar notion, deliverance from hell, or going to heaven; but a present deliverance from sin, a restoration of the soul to its primitive health, its original purity; a recovery of the divine nature; the renewal of our souls after the image of God, in righteousness and true holiness, in justice, mercy, and truth. This implies all holy and heavenly tempers, and, by consequence, all holiness of conversation. Now, if by salvation we mean a present salvation from sin, we cannot say, holiness is the condition of it; for it is the thing itself. Salvation, in this sense, and holiness, are synonymous terms. We must affirm always, 'We are saved by faith.' Faith is the sole

---

[81]   *Sermon 43, The Scripture Way of Salvation, Works,* Vol. 2, p. 156.

condition of this salvation. For without faith we
cannot be thus saved. But whosoever believeth is
saved already. [82]

The key phrase here is 'a restoration of the soul to primitive heath'. In Wesley salvation is therapeutic, rather than forensic, and therefore debates about whether justification is imputed or imparted tend to pass us by, as they emotionally and existentially passed Wesley by. As we saw in our brief discussion of 'Aldersgatism' earlier, Wesley's life long concern was 'sanctification' rather than justification. His note in his *Journal* for May 24th, 'I think it was about five this morning, that I opened my Testament on these words [he quotes them first in Greek] "There are given to us exceeding great and precious promises, even that ye should be partakers of the divine nature,"' reminds us of Wesley's strong commitment to the Eastern Fathers, for whom *theosis*, 'becoming what God is' is the supreme image of salvation. Christ in this tradition became what we are that we might become what he is and share his life. Sacramental theology begins to speak of the *pharmakon anthanasias,* the medicine of immortality or which leads to immortality.

This is a real clue to Wesleyan theology. As a loyal Anglican John Wesley accepted completely the Reformation formula: 'we are accounted righteous before God only for the merit of our Lord and Saviour, faith, and not for our merits or deserving. Wherefore, that we are justified by faith is a most wholesome doctrine, and very full of comfort, as is more largely expressed in the Homily of Justification.'[83]   He assented to this doctrine when he was ordained and had preached it before May 1938. To be sure

---

[82]   *A Farther Appeal to Men of Religion and Reason, Works* , Vol. 11, p. 162.
[83]   No. XI of the *Articles of Religion* of the Church of England, no.IX of the Articles of Religion of the Methodist Church.

Luther's *Preface to the Romans* enabled him to attain a deep personal sense of forgiveness at about a quarter before nine on May 24th, 1738. But this sense of forgiveness was but a part of what he was always seeking. His search was for a full and complete holiness, which has to include a 'Spirit of power', which would both indwell and heal. Charles Wesley understood his brother's purpose and wrote magnificently of 'finished holiness' as 'salvation' and salvation as 'finished holiness':

> O come and dwell in me,
> Spirit of power within,
> And bring the glorious liberty
> From sorrow, fear, and sin.
> The seed of sin's disease
> Spirit of health, remove,
> Spirit of finished holiness,
> Spirit of perfect love.[84]

In Wesleyan theology we never say holiness is the condition of salvation: holiness is salvation itself, and holiness is health.

2. No Salvation Pessimism: Salvation is for Everyone

Wesley's eighteenth century world was inhabited by many who had drunk deeply of the wells of Augustine and John Calvin. Augustine wrote in *The City of God* (probably the most influential theological volume of all time): 'many more are left under punishment than are delivered from it, in order that it may be shown what was due to all.'[85] The Baptist theologian, Clark H. Pinnock calls such a senti-

---

[84] *A Collection of Hymns for the Use of the People Called Methodists*, 1780, No. 356, *Works*, Vol 7, p.525; *Hymns and Psalms*, No. 293.
[85] Book 21 Chapter 12.

ment a 'pessimism of salvation.'[86] 'With Augustine,' he goes on, 'a new and severe paradigm in theology was born, a package of dismal beliefs which would eat its way into the consciousness of Western churches and erode the positive biblical spirit in their thinking.' Both Luther and Calvin were heirs of Augustine in their gloomy views about the bondage of the will and the impossibility of human achievement without all-enabling grace. Calvin went on to develop the Augustinian theology in his doctrine of predestination:

> The covenant of life is not preached equally to all, and among those to whom it is preached, does not always meet with the same reception. This diversity displays the unsearchable depth of the divine judgment, and is without doubt subordinate to God's purpose of divine election.[87]

Scholastic or hyper-Calvinism went much further than Calvin, and is manifested in such works as the *Lambeth Articles* of 1596 and the *Westminster Confession* of 1647, both of which were extremely well known to John Wesley. But since they are hardly known at all to late twentieth-century Christians in Britain (in America there are many Christians who know precisely whether they are five point Calvinists or thirteen point Calvinists), it may be as well to give some sense of their flavour. First from the *Lambeth Articles:*

> 1. God from eternity has predestinated certain men unto life: certain men he hath reprobated. 2. The moving or efficient cause of predestination unto life is not the foresight of faith, or of perseverance, or of

---

86 *A Wideness in God's Mercy: the Finality of Jesus Christ in a World of Religion,* Zondervan, 1992, pp. 37-9.

87 *Institutes of the Christian Religion* (transl, Henry Beveridge), John Clarke, 1962, vol. 2. p. 202.

good works ... but only the good will and pleasure of God.
3. There is predetermined a certain number of the predestinate, which can neither be augmented nor diminished. 4. Those who are not predestinated to salvation shall be necessarily damned for their sins. 5. A true living and justifying faith, and a sanctifying by the Spirit of God is not extinguished ... it vanisheth not away in the elect, either finally or totally. 6. A man ... who is endued with justifying faith is certain, with the full assurance of faith, of the remission off his sins, and of his everlasting salvation by Christ. 7. Saving grace is ... not granted, not communicated to all men, by which they may be saved if they will. 8. No man can come unto Christ unless it shall be given unto him, and unless the Father shall draw him; and all men are not drawn by the Father, that they may come to the Son. 9. It is not in the will or power of every one to be saved. [88]

These sentiments can be compared with two samples from the *Westminster Confession* (from the Scots 1647 version.) First from the last part of Chapter XII, 'Of Effectual Calling':

> Others, not elected, though they may be called by the ministry of the word, and may have some common operations of the Spirit, yet they never truly come to Christ, and therefore cannot be saved; much less can men, not professing the Christian religion, be saved in any other way whatsoever be they never so diligent to frame their lives according to the light of nature, and the law of that religion they do profess; and to assert that they may is very pernicious and to be detested.

And second, from the last section of Chapter XVIII, 'Of Good Works',

> Works done by unregenerate men, although for the matter of them they may be things which God com-

---

[88] The *Lambeth Articles* can be found in Philip Schaff, *Creeds of Christendom*, Vol. 3, pp.523-24

mands, and of good use both to themselves and to others; yet because they proceed not from a heart purified by faith; nor yet are done in a right manner, according to the word; nor a right end, the glory of God; they are therefore sinful, and cannot please God or make a man meet to receive grace from God.[89]

The implications of these mournful views were not lost on Wesley's contemporaries. Just two examples will suffice. When Wesley was still an infant, in 1705, Joseph Hussey (1660-1726), a Presbyterian preacher in Cambridge, published his *God's Operations of Grace but No Offers of Grace*, in which he asserted that 'offers rob the Gospel of its properties, privileges and glory', so that grace should only be offered to those for whom it was intended. As Wesley's long life drew to a close, William Carey was locked in a struggle to persuade his own denomination, the Particular Baptists, that there could indeed be not only 'offers of grace' but, even more, Christians were under an 'obligation to use means for the conversion of the heathen' and therefore to set up a missionary society. In this battle, he had the support of Andrew Fuller, who published his *The Gospel Worthy of All Acceptation* in 1785. Even so, in that same year, J.C. Ryland could rebuke William Carey in the true voice of hyper-Calvinism: 'Sit down, young man; when God wants to convert the heathen, He'll do it without your help or mine'.

Hussey and Fuller symbolise for us the one theme that Wesley returned to again and again in his practical theological writings, and which made him entitle his periodical

---

[89] With this should be compared Article XIII of the Anglican *Articles of Religion*, "f Works done before Justification': it is to be noted that Wesley omitted this in his list of XXIV Articles for the U.S. Methodist Church.

for the Methodist people *The Arminian Magazine* [90] In the preface to its first volume, Wesley declared that purpose of the periodical was to set forth 'that grand Christian doctrine "God willeth all men to be saved and to come to the knowledge of the truth" 1 Tim 4.10.'

The Arminian Magazine was indeed a propagandist work. Here is Charles Wesley's polemic verse as printed in the October, 1788 issue. It is entitled *OF GOD'S EVER-LASTING LOVE*

1   Father whose everlasting love
Thy only Son for sinners gave,
Whose Grace to All did freely move,
And sent Him down a world to save

2   Help us thy Mercy to extol
 Immense, unfathom'd, unconfined;
To praise the Lamb who died for all,
 The general Saviour of mankind.

3   Thy undistinguishing Regard
Was cast on Adam's fallen race;
For all Thou hast in Christ prepared,
Sufficient, sovereign, saving Grace.

4   Jesus hath said, we all shall hope,
Preventing Grace for all is free
"I, if I be lifted up,
I will draw All Men unto Me."

5   What those drawings never knew?
With whom hath not thy Spirit strove?
We all must own that God is true
We all may feel that God is Love.

---

[90]   In honour of Jacobus Arminius who had challenged Dutch scholastic Calvinism in 1610. His *Remonstrance* affirmed 1) election is conditional and is dependent upon God's foreknowledge of personal faith, 2) Christ died for all 3) No one can exercise saving faith unless regeneration by the Holy Spirit has taken place 4) Grace, while indispensable to the Christian life, is not irresistible. 5) The Final Perseverance of all believers is very doubtful. This challenge had led to the Synod of Dort (1618-9) which redefined Calvinism under five headings: teaching total depravity, unconditional election, limited atonement, irresistible grace, and the final perseverance of the saints.

6   O all ye ends of earth behold
The bleeding, all-atoning Lamb!
Look unto Him for sinners sold,
Look and be saved thro' Jesu's name.

7   Behold the lamb of God, who takes
The sins of all the world away.
His pity no exception makes;
But all that *will receive* Him, *may.*

8   A world he suffer'd to redeem;
For all He hath the atonement made;
For those that will not come to Him
The Ransom of his life was paid.

9   Their Lord unto his own He came;
His own were who received Him not,
Denied and trampled on his name,
And blood, by which themselves were bought.

10   Who under foot their Saviour trod,
 Expose'd afresh and crucified,
Who trampled on the Son of God,
For them, for them, their Saviour died.

11   For those who at the judgement-day
On Him they pierc'd shall look with pain;
The Lamb for every cast-away,
For every soul of man was slain.

12   Why then, Thou Universal Love,
Should any of thy Grace despair?
To all thy Bowels move,
But straitned in our own we are.

13   'Tis we, the wretched abjects we
Our blasphemies on Thee translate;
We think that Fury is in Thee,
Horribly think, that God is hate!

14   "Thou hast compell'd the lost to die,
Hath reprobated from thy face;
Hath others sav'd, by them past by;
Or mock'd with only *Damning Grace.*"

15 How long, Thou Jealous God! How long
Shall impious worms thy word disprove,
Thy justice slay, thy Mercy wrong,
Deny thy Faithfulness and Love?

16 Still shall the Hellish Doctrine stand?
And Thee for its dire Author claim?
No -- let it sink, at thy command,
Down to the pit from whence it came.

17 Arise O God, maintain thy Cause!
The Fulness of the Gentiles call:
Lift up the standard of thy cross,
And all shall own thou diedst for All.
     * More usually call'd *Common Grace*.[91]

Here is doctrine put into verse with considerable force.
Compilers of Methodist hymnody have balked at asking
this to be used in public worship (it was never part of the
*Collection of Hymns for the Use of the People Called
Methodists,* 1780), and British Methodists are invited to
sing only verses 1-3, 5 and 17 in *Hymns and Psalms.* The
other verses speak for themselves, and make sense only in
the context of the *Lambeth Articles* and the *Westminster
Confession.*

Of course this polemic takes other forms. We noted already that the *Explanatory Notes on the New Testament*
had their root cause in Wesley's desire to ensure that the
New Testament be read in an Arminian way. This, for example, is Wesley's commentary on 1 Timothy 2, verses 3-
7

> *Verse 3   For this* -- that we pray for all men. Do
> you ask, 'Why are not more converted?' We do not
> pray enough. *Is acceptable in the sight of God our
> Saviour* -- Who has actually saved us that believe,
> and *willeth all men to be saved.* It is strange that

---

[91] *The Arminian Magazine*, October 1788, pp. 430-31, emphases in the original.

any whom he has actually saved should doubt the universality of his grace! Verse *4 who willeth seriously all men* -- Not a part only, much less the smallest part. *To be saved* -- eternally. This treated of, verses 5, 6. *And,* in order thereto, *to come* -- They are not compelled. *To the knowledge of the truth* -- Which brings salvation. This treated of, verses 6,7.

But perhaps someone will ask: 'is not all this Arminian/Calvinist debate a dead issue; a story of battles past and long ago? How can all this disputation be relevant to any formulation of 'classical Christianity'? There are two answers to these objections.

The first has a slight overtone of triumphalism, because it suggests that the Methodist-Arminian view became the orthodoxy of later Protestantism. Certainly other factors and other personalities were involved in the revolt against Calvinism in the nineteenth century. [92] But it would not be unfair to claim that the theological presuppositions which lay at the heart of the Methodist movement influenced all other evangelistic movements to the detriment of Calvinist orthodoxy. In the nineteenth century, the Methodist theologian Thomas Jackson asked John Cockin, a L.M.S. missionary, why he was going to the unbelieving world if he believed that Christ did not die for all. Cockin replied that Calvinists like himself made 'the decree of election as extensive as actual salvation' and that therefore in their plan 'the multitude of the redeemed is as great at yours, but our peculiarity is to ascribe their final happiness to discriminatory mercy and special grace'. But his colleagues in the London Missionary Society soon came to agree with their fellow Congregationalist (and founder of the Evangelical Union in Scotland) John Morrison, 'Men need not go to

---

[92]   For this see my *Justice Courtesy and Love*, pp. 20-27.

heathen lands with the doctrine of a limited atonement in their creed, or, if they go with it, they must hide it.'[93]   In 1879 the Declaratory Act made the beliefs of the Westminster Confession optional for Scottish Presbyterians. Historian A.C. Cheyne called this change of heart 'nothing less than Victorian Scotland's religious revolution', and the same kind of changes may be traced elsewhere.[94]   This means that generally speaking Methodists are no longer entrammelled in such controversies with our friends of mainstream Baptist, Congregationalist and Presbyterian traditions.[95]

But the issues are not altogether out of sight and out of mind. We have referred already to the dangers of that retrenchment in Christian thinking which postulates seventeenth century Puritanism as 'classical Christianity' We may take as an example J.I. Packer's *A Quest for Godliness: the Puritan Vision of the Christian Life*.[96]   Packer has some unsatisfactory comments on the relation of five-point Calvinism to evangelism, in which he suggests that all sermons ought to be evangelistic, since there is no way of knowing who is listening. Methodists, however, would look back on their history and suggest that when all sermons in general are evangelistic, none is in particular. There needs to be a deliberate intentionality in reaching beyond the gathered congregation. Methodists would also suspect that even sermons which are deliberately evangelistic but are delivered in a church building, will reach only persons who have some basic understanding of the Christian faith. Neither Packer nor the Puritan Divines have

---

[93]   These quotations may be found in *Justice Courtesy and Love* pp. 23 and 301-2.

[94]   I have tried to this in *Justice, Courtesy and Love, passim*.

[95]   These controversies have not gone away over wide tracts of America, and Princeton orthodoxy still hold the minds of hearts of many people: the works of Charles Hodge are always in print.

[96]   Crossway Books, 1990, pp. 165-7.

much conception of evangelism as cross-cultural communication of the Gospel, or much that is helpful to say about it. A normative and prescriptive theology should be conscious always of the great part of the world's population who understand very little of language and terminology of the Christian faith, and who are complete strangers to its background and culture.

Thus the Wesleyan conception of unrestricted, boundless grace impinges directly upon the task of evangelism in a culturally and religiously plural world. In the Methodist version of 'classical Christianity', we encourage each other to sing.

> What shall I do my God to love
> My loving God to praise?
> The length, and breadth and height to prove
> And depth of sovereign grace.
>
> Thy sovereign grace to all extends,
> Immense and Unconfined,
> From age to age it never ends;
> It reaches all mankind.
>
> Throughout the world its breadth is known,
> Wide as infinity;
> So wide it never passed by one,
> Or it had passed by me.[97]

If this all-extensive sovereign grace means anything at all it has to be more than common grace (which is in the Wesleyan view, as we saw, merely 'damning grace' and therefore a mockery). It must mean that grace touches positively all human lives.

---

[97] *Hymns and Psalms* , No. 46, cf. the very similar hymn 'What shall I do my God to love? My Saviour and the world's to praise?' *Hymns and Psalms*, No.47, and *A Collection of Hymns for the Use of the People Called Methodists*, 1780, No 367, p. 536.

3. All people are already graced

Because Wesley was not tied to scholastic formulas he could propose another understanding of the human person. This went beyond scholastic formulations of the relationship between nature and grace.[98] For Wesley, grace is not an entity or substance introduced into human beings to perfect their fallen natures. Much rather grace is the Holy Spirit, the very life of God within human beings and as such is all pervasive, and certainly prevenient. As Cobb writes 'human beings do not first exist in separation from God and then come into a relationship with God. Their very life is already God's presence within them.'[99] So, too, their knowledge of God, and their ability to do good, is the very life of God within them. John Wesley repeatedly stated this. Here are just three examples. 'No man living is without some preventing grace, and every degree of grace is a degree of life';[100] '[In] some sense it may be said to every child of man: "He hath showed thee O man, what is good; even to do justly, to love mercy and walk humbly with thy God." With this truth he has in some measure, "enlightened everyone that cometh into this world"[101]; and, again, in his *Explanatory Notes* on John 1.9 *'This was the true Light, which lighteth every man that cometh into the world'* - By what is vulgarly termed natural conscience, pointing at least the general lines of good and evil. And this light, if man did not hinder, would shine more and more to the perfect day.' [102]

Prevenient grace in Wesleyan understanding is thus very far removed from 'common grace' or 'natural theology' -

---

[98] For a succinct summary of the issues here see John B. Cobb, *op.cit*, pp. 35-55.

[99] *Ibid*, p.40.

[100] *Letter to John Mason*, (Nov. 21, 1776) *Works*, Vol. 6. p. 239.

[101] *Sermon 85 On Working out our own Salvation* , Works, Vol. 3, pp. 199-20.

[102] *Explanatory Notes*, ad loc.

that limited reflection of the remains of God's image in human beings which were intended, in Augustinian/Calvinist, understandings for the restraining of evil. Prevenient grace in Wesleyan understanding is teleological, loaded with divine intentionality. It is all about God's purpose in saving humankind.

Furthermore 'prevenience' is not a stage of grace, some part of a putative Wesleyan *order of salvation* (first prevenient grace, then real grace!), but is rather the crucial aspect of grace in all its manifestations. It signifies the divine initiative in all spirituality, in all Christian experience, among all people. It is at once the work of Christ and the work of the Spirit.

Because God's love is so graciously 'immanent and active in human life,'[103] Methodists affirm every person as loved by God and capable of response to God. This doctrine is invaluable to pastors and to counsellors who know that teachings of human depravity and reprobation make no sense as 'gospel' to people lost in self-deprecation and self-contempt. It is of equal importance to missionaries concerned with the fatalistic emphases of some eastern religious traditions. Teachings of, for example, original sin, total depravity, the abiding wrath of God and universal condemnation, are not 'good news', nor can they ever be, to those whose spirits are subdued by karmic fatalism or the *kismet* of Islamic folk religion.

The implications of the universality of God's grace were not lost on John Wesley. For him Christ must surely work even in those who do not hear the Gospel in this life. The final destiny of so many ('five parts of mankind out of six are totally ignorant of Christianity') who had never heard

---

103   Albert C. Outler (ed.), *John Wesley,* p. 33.

the gospel was as real a question for Wesley as for Augustine and Calvin. His first instinct was to avoid any implication that the lost ones were created for damnation. Then, he said, any judgment can be left to the mercy of God, because in his words 'I have no authority from the Word of God to "judge those who are without."' Nor could he conceive that any one has a right to sentence the heathen and Mohametan world to damnation. 'It is far better to leave them to Him who made them.'[104]

But his most important answer lay in the implications of 'prevenient grace.' Those who lived before Christ, those who live out the frameworks of Christianity are accounted acceptable to God through their response the promptings of the natural conscience. But, as we have just heard, natural conscience is for Wesley more properly termed 'preventing grace.' For him, as the Sri Lankan Methodist Wesley Ariarajah explains, people 'who have not yet had the opportunity of hearing the gospel, yet have responded to prevenient grace, are, like the patriarchs, justified by faith in anticipation of the revelation of Christ.' [105]

In our own religiously plural world, Wesleyan theology enables us to recognise that everyone we have to deal with is touched by this preveniency of grace, the Holy Spirit already at work their lives, however much they try to deny or extinguish it. That God is already at work through the Holy Spirit is even more so in the case of the saints and sages, believers and devotees whose love and devotion to God are expressed in different ways from that of Christians. Thus the many Methodist theologians present in the WCC Consultation on Religious Plurality in Baar, Swit-

---

[104] *Sermon* 130, *On Living without God, Works* Vol. 4. p. 174.
[105] 'Evangelism and Wesley's Catholicity of Grace', in M. Douglas Meeks (ed.), *op.cit,* p. 144.

zerland, January, 1990, joined company with Orthodox and Roman Catholics there in affirming of other world religious traditions,

> that God has been present in their seeking and their finding, that where there is truth and wisdom in their teaching, and love and holiness in their living, this like any wisdom, insight, knowledge, understanding, love and holiness that is found amongst us is the fruit of the Holy Spirit. We also affirm that God is with them as they struggle along with us for justice and liberation.[106]

Wesley Ariarajah, for many years Director of the Dialogue Unit of the WCC and then its Associate General Secretary, sees the evangelistic task in this context as inviting men and women to move 'from grace to grace.'[107] He continues: 'Some would argue that such a generous doctrine of grace would undercut the urgency in evangelism. Wesley's own life remains the answer to this objection, for the same Wesley who held this doctrine of universal grace was also the greatest evangelist of his time.'[108]

4. All forgiveness is of grace

The prevenience of grace has as its absolute presupposition the understanding of God, Father, Son and Holy Spirit, the Triune God of Christian faith. For John Wesley there could be no time B.C., 'before Christ', because Christ was with the Father before all worlds, 'God of God' and 'Light of Light' and 'True God of true God.' The world was created therefore in grace, and this means in the redemptive love of the 'lamb slain before the foundations of the world.' So while his expression of the doctrine of original

---

[106] In Michael Kinnamon and Brian E Cope (eds.), *The Ecumenical Movement: An Anthology of Key Texts and Voices,* WCC, 1997, p. 418.
[107] *Op.cit*, pp. 144 .
[108] *Ibid.*

sin was usually in the severest terms ("'through the offence of one" all are dead, dead to God, dead in sin, dwelling in a corruptible, mortal body, shortly to be dissolved and under a sentence of death') and while he taught that total depravity was the result of the fall, there is no sense of the tyranny of Genesis 3 (in which theology starts from 'the sinful man' rather than from the grace of God) in authentic Wesleyan forms of theology.

Redemption in Wesleyan theology is often seen as a divine remedial action after the fall had taken place, so that Adam's transgression could be described as a 'happy fault' (*felix culpa*). In creation, God was already at work with and through redeeming grace. This high Trinitarian doctrine of prevenient grace, in Colin Williams's words, 'broke the chain of logical necessity by which Calvin's doctrine of predestination seems to flow from the doctrine of original sin.'[109]   But, as much as in Luther or Calvin,[110] justifying grace has to act within the sinful personality before the new life can begin, and this is focussed upon the work of Christ on the cross:

> And can it be that I should gain
> An interest in the Saviour's blood?
> Died he for me, who caused his pain,
> For me? Who him to death pursued?[111]

Justification and the new birth are to be seen as the indispensable beginnings of a total change of life and character.

---

[109] *John Wesley's Theology Today*, p. 44.

[110]   'Q, Wherein do we come to the very edge of Calvinism? A. In ascribing all good to the free grace of God. (2.) In denying natural free will, and all power antecedent to grace. And (3.) In excluding all merit from man; even for what he has or does by the grace of God' *Minutes*, 1745.

[111]   A *Collection of Hymns for the Use of the People Called Methodists*, 1780, No 193, p. 322. Henry Bett offered the suggestion that the author of this hymn was John, not Charles, see *The Hymns of Methodism*, Epworth, 1945, p. 26.

Long my imprisoned spirit lay,
Fast bound in sin and nature's night,
Thine eye diffused a quick'ning ray;
I woke; the dungeon flamed with light,
My chains fell of, my heart was free,
I rose went forth and followed thee.[112]

Therefore, through faith, through grace, there is no condemnation to be dreaded. We are made alive in Christ our living head, and in the words of this same hymn, 'clothed in righteousness divine'. Now we can move to that transformation of mind and temper that is salvation.

6. Grace transforms to the uttermost

The work of the Holy Spirit preoccupies Methodists as much as that of the work of Christ.[113] This is manifest in the hymns of both brothers. John Wesley radically altered some verses by Henry More (1614-87), the Cambridge Platonist, to give his people this striking hymn (the first verse is by Wesley himself):

On all the earth thy Spirit shower;
The earth in righteousness renew;
Thy kingdom come, and hell's o'erpower;
And to thy sceptre all subdue.

Like mighty wind or torrent fierce,
Let it opposers all o'errun;
And every law of sin reverse,
That faith and love may make all one.

Yea, let thy Spirit in every place,
Its richer energy declare;

---

112   *Ibid* p. 323.
113   With grace as its axial theme Methodist theology is Christocentric, but never Christomonistic. Because of its rooted Trinitarianism, Methodist theology is 'just as equally Pneumatological as Christocentric.' Cf. Albert Outler, 'A New Future for Wesley Studies: an Agenda for "Phase III"', in M. Douglas Meeks, *op.cit.* p. 44.

While lovely tempers, fruits of grace,
The kingdom of thy Christ prepare.[114]

The insights of these verses lead in two directions. There is the transformation of the individual in personal holiness, but equally there is the transformation of world in the destruction of all that prevents 'lovely tempers, fruits of grace.' Wesleyans sensed that they had to eradicate what would be called today 'structural' or 'systemic' sins: the slave trade, alcohol and drug trafficking, inadequate education, unavailability of credit to the poor, the exploitation of children. From the beginnings of Methodism, Wesley and his followers sought to offer physical and psychological healing as well as other-worldly salvation. Both healing and salvation, synonymous themselves, are implicit in the synonyms for Wesley's central doctrine: entire sanctification, perfect love, Christian perfection, and scriptural holiness.

To be sure many Wesleyans have laid more emphasis on the first of these terms, 'entire sanctification,' which they have often understood in a completely individualistic sense. They have some right on their side, for no one would question that the concern for the entire transformation of the human person is a wholly proper and Biblical emphasis. Wesley makes this clear through his comments on Colossians, Ch. 3:

> Verse 12. All who are thus renewed are elected of God holy, and therefore beloved of him. Holiness is the consequence of their election and God's superior love, of their holiness. Verse 13, *Forbearing one another* -- if anything is now wrong. *And forgiving one another* -- what is past. Verse 14. The love of God contains the whole of Christian perfection, and

---

[114]   *A Collection of Hymns for the Use of the People Called Methodists*, 1780, No 445, p. 624; *Hymns and Psalms* No. 321.

> connects all the parts of it together. Verse 15. And
> then the peace of God shall rule in your hearts --
> Shall sway every temper, affection, thought, as the
> reward (so the Greek word implies) of your pre-
> ceding love and obedience.

But there has been much confusion in Methodist ranks about one element in this 'Christian perfection.' Wesley's own many and varied ruminations about the possibility of this gift of holiness being received instantaneously was inordinately confusing to many of his followers both in Britain and in America.[115] Salvationist, Holiness, and Pentecostalist movements have so emphasised this teaching as to have separated from mainstream Wesleyanism, and in so doing, as many think, have lost the full-orbed splendour of Methodist theology.[116] But the abuse never takes away the use, and it is still vitally important to insist that deeply embedded in Methodist theology is a sense that God can change the situation of an individual man or woman so that there is no barrier caused by sin, guilt, fear or shame, and that he or she can be lost in wonder, love and praise.

Wesley's own teaching goes no further than that. Certainly he never indicated that perfection implied freedom from

---

[115] For two splendid attempts to unravel some of the confusion see two articles in Vinson Synan (ed.), *Aspects of Pentecostalist-Charismatic Origins,* Logos International, 1975 by members of the Wesleyan Church. The first by Donald W. Dayton discusses the movement 'From Christian Perfection to "the Baptism of the Holy Ghost"', pp. 41-54. The second by Melvin E. Dieter is a graphic description of 'The Wesleyan Holiness Aspects of Pentecostal Origins: as Mediated through the Nineteenth Century Holiness Revival.' pp. 55-80.

[116] It is very important to note that the most searching criticisms of the Wesleyan Holiness traditions have recently been coming from within Holiness circles themselves. Cf. this statement by Floyd Cunningham, a theological teacher from the Church of the Nazarene: 'A Wesleyan renaissance in the 1960's began to distinguish between Wesleyan and American holiness movement roots with the result that Wesley was reclaimed as chief theologian'. He continues, 'with the recovery of Wesley came also a renewed understanding of grace and especially prevenient grace'. He points especially to the work of Mildred Bangs Wyncoop and her important book we have already cited. Cunningham comments on excessive pneumatocenticity in 'baptism with the Holy Spirit language', *op.cit.* p. 204.

ignorance, mistakes, temptations, and the thousand infirmities necessarily connected with flesh and blood. He did, on the other hand, insist that there is a perfection in 'loving God with all our heart and mind and soul', that it was possible that the God of Peace would sanctify us wholly; and that we should 'be preserved entire, without blame, at the coming of our Lord Jesus Christ' (1 Thess. 5. 23). Perfect love names a goal which the Christian individual can reach even in the present life. The power to open ourselves to perfecting grace is not in ourselves and our own moral strength. It rests with the work of God's Spirit with us. But potentiality may become actuality through grace and that is what Wesleyans preach: 'I can do all things in Him that strengtheneth me' (Phil. 4.13).[117]

So the first step is to turn towards Christ. Charles Wesley wrote twelve lines that perfectly encapsulate the process:

> Jesus the First and Last.
> On thee my soul is cast;
> Thou didst the work begin
> By blotting out my sin
> Thou wilt the root remove,
> And perfect me in love.
>
> Yet when the work is done,
> The work is but begun'
> Partaker of thy grace'
> I long to see thy face
> The first I prove below.
> The last I die to know.[118]

---

[117]   And so of course do Calvinists: see Ronald S. Wallace, *Calvin's Doctrine of the Christian Life*, Oliver and Boyd, 1959. Geoffrey Wainwright helpfully compares Wesleyan and Calvinist understandings in his chapter 'Perfect Salvation in the Teaching of Wesley and Calvin,' in *Methodists in Dialog*, pp. 143-158.

[118]   *Hymns and Psalms* No. 736 Eric W. Baker thought that this hymn encapsulated the Wesleyan doctrine of grace unto perfection, see *The Faith of a Methodist*, Epworth, 1958, pp. 108-112 .

Along with this sense of individual pilgrimage, authentic Wesleyanism has another dream, a dream of a transformed society, when Scriptural holiness shall be spread 'throughout the land' (British tradition) or 'over these lands' (American tradition). This is how Wesley himself dreamed it, as set out his Sermon on *Scriptural Christianity:*

> Suppose now the fullness of time to be come, and the prophecies to be accomplished. What a prospect is this! ... Wars are ceased from the earth ... no brother rising up against brother; no country or city divided against itself, and tearing out its own bowels. ... Here is no oppression to "make" even "the wise man mad;" no extortion to "grind the face of the poor;" no robbery or wrong; no rapine or injustice; for all are "content with such things as they possess." Thus "righteousness and peace have kissed each other;" (Psalm 85:10) they have "taken root and filled the land;" "righteousness flourishing out of the earth," and "peace looking down from heaven."

> And with righteousness, or justice, mercy is also found. The earth is no longer full of cruel habitations. ... And being filled with peace and joy in believing, and united in one body, by one Spirit, they all love as brethren, they are all of one heart, and of one soul. "Neither saith any of them, that aught of the things which he possesseth is his own." There is none among them that lacketh; for every man loveth his neighbour as himself and all walk by one rule: "Whatever ye would that men should do unto you, even so do unto them."

> It follows, that no unkind word can ever be heard among them, no strife of tongues, no contention of any kind, no railings or evil-speaking; but every one "opens his mouth with wisdom, and in his tongue there is the law of kindness." Equally incapable are they of fraud or guile: Their love is without dissimulation: Their words are always the just expression of their thoughts, opening a window into their

breast, that whosoever desires may look into their
hearts, and see that only love and God are there.[119]

Charles Wesley puts this into verse:

> Come then to thy servants again,
> Who long thy appearing to know;
> Thy quiet and peaceable reign
> In mercy establish below;
> All sorrow before thee shall fly,
> And anger and malice be o'er,
> And envy and malice shall die,
> And discord afflict us no more. [120]

To this vision great numbers of Wesleyans have been intensely loyal. The eagerness with which Methodists have
embraced on both sides of the Atlantic, and then throughout the world, first 'the social gospel' and later 'liberation
theology' can be traced to this vision of 'social righteousness.' As one of them (Hugh Price Hughes) once re-
marked, 'there is no holiness without social holiness.'

 Speaking of the doctrine of Perfect Love in 1927, that
great teacher of Methodist doctrine Henry Maldwyn
Hughes, the first principal of Wesley House, declared that
this was:

> part of her commission to which Methodism is not
> bearing adequate witness. There is need to sound
> anew the note that there are no limits to the possi-
> bilities of growth in the Christian life and that
> Christian men and women should not be satisfied
> with moral or spiritual mediocrity. The expression
> 'entire sanctification' is capable of a wider applica-
> tion than has been commonly given to it, namely the

---

119 *Sermon 4, Scriptural Christianity, Works*, Vol.1 p.171.
120 *Hymns and Psalms* , No. 400.

sanctification of social life in every part, the baptism of all departments of life into the Spirit of Christ, and the bringing of every sphere and relationship into the captivity of his obedience. This also is to achieved by Perfect Love.[121]

As one of Maldwyn Hughes' later successors, I need add only that this judgement remains in force in 1998.

---

[121]   *Christian Foundations,* Epworth, 1927, pp. 164-5.

Chapter Four
The Catholic Spirit and Religious Reality

We have seen that the sense that all human life is lived within the framework of prevenient grace enabled Wesley to be far more optimistic about the salvation of other men and women than most of his predecessors in the Christian theological traditions of the West. Two other elements, as well as prevenient grace, can be discerned in John Wesley's attitudes toward those who are outside the Christian framework. There is first a realistic 'common sense' in discerning both goodness outside Christianity and evil within it. The second is, as we have seen, an incipient recognition of what we would call today a Logos Christology.

The first is perhaps a non-theological factor. His eighteenth century 'common sense' or 'reasonableness' which made him so attractive a figure to people like Samuel Johnson, manifested itself both when he read his Bible and in his routine encounters with people who were other than Christians. A vivid Biblical example is to found in the *Explanatory Notes*, on Mark 9.39ff. Wesley is discussing the outrage of the disciples because they had found a man casting out demons in the name of Jesus:

> *Jesus said* -- Christ here gives us a lovely example of candour and moderation. He was willing to put the best construction upon doubtful cases, and treat as friends those who were not avowed enemies. Perhaps in this instance it was means of conquering the remainder of prejudice and perfecting what was wanting in the faith and obedience of these persons.

> *Forbid him not* -- Neither directly nor indirectly discourage any man who brings sinners from the power of Satan to God, "because he followeth not us," in opinions, modes of worship, or anything else which does not affect the essence of religion.[122]

This verse is also the text of one of Wesley's most effective sermons, the famous *Sermon* 28, *Caution Against Bigotry*,[123] which contains his definition of bigotry: 'too strong an attachment to, or fondness for, our own party, opinion, Church, and religion.' Perhaps this is not after all a non-theological factor, but an announcement of the duty of Christians to see things as they really are, and not to prejudge where the presence of God might be manifested. An example of Wesley's own lack of bigotry and ability to see things for what they are comes in this story of an encounter with the Jewish people. 'I was desired', he writes, 'to hear Mr. Leoui sing at the Jewish synagogue. I never before saw a Jewish congregation behave so decently. Indeed the place itself is so solemn, that it might strike an awe upon those who have any thought of God.'[124]

But my favourite example of Wesley's ability to take in the facts as they are, comes in an incident he recounts in his *Sermon* 106, *On Faith*. Wesley had read, either in a Latin or an English translation, an Arabic novel ('this story seems to be feigned', he says) about a castaway on a desert island.[125] In this novel, its protagonist, Hai Ebn Yokdan, worked out all by himself the main outlines of theism and ethics (this story also gave Daniel Defoe the idea for *Robinson Crusoe*). So Wesley writes:

---

122   *Explanatory Notes*, ad loc.
123   *Works*, Vol. 2 p 67
124   *Journal* , February 23rd, 1769. *ad loc*
125   The Arabic text of the *Life of Hay ibn Yakzam* had appeared with a Latin translation in 1691, under the title *Philosophicus Autodidactus*. An English translation of this had appeared in 1708, and was reprinted several times during Wesley's lifetime.

> But many of them (i.e., the ancient Heathens), espe-
> cially in the civilised nations, we have great reason
> to hope, although they lived among heathens, yet
> were quite of another spirit; being taught of God, by
> his inward voice, all the essentials of true religion.
> Yea, so was that Mohametan, and Arabian, who, a
> century or two ago, wrote the Life of Hai Ebn Yok-
> dan. The story seems to be feigned; but it contains
> all the principles of pure religion and undefiled.[126]

Two things are happening here. Despite all the eighteenth
century prejudices about the people who were called 'Mahometans,'[127] John Wesley was able to see Islam as a
form of true religion. But notice also that he had no hesitation in discerning direct communication from God ('being
taught of God, by his inward voice').

This is consistent with all that we have seen about
Wesley's understanding of the presence of the Word (or
Christ) in prevenient grace. I quote now in full the passage
in the *Explanatory Notes* from which we have already
taken a couple of sentences:

> 4. *In him was life* - he was the foundation of life to
> every living thing, as well as of being to all that is. -
> He is essential life and the Giver of life to all that li-
> veth, was also the light of men, the fountain of wis-
> dom, holiness and happiness to man in his original
> state. 5 *And the light shineth in the darkness* - Shines
> even on fallen man - *But the darkness* -- dark, sinful
> man -- *perceiveth it not* ... 7. *[John] came to testify
> of the light* --- *Of Christ.* 9. who lighteth every man -
> - by what is vulgarly called natural conscience,
> pointing out at least the general lines of good and

---

126   Sermon 106, *On Faith, Works*, Vol . 3, p. 494 .

127   See for example Charles Wesley's expression of these attitudes in *A Collection
of Hymns for the People Called Methodists*, No. 431, 'For the Mahometans' with its
typical view of Mohammed: 'The Unitarian fiend expel/And chase his doctrine back to
hell'. *Works*, Vol, 7, p. 431.

evil. And this light, if man did not hinder, would shine more and more to the perfect day.

This is surely the basis for a Logos Christology.

a catholic spirit and the religion of the heart

Perhaps the most influential Sermon he ever set out for the edification of his Methodist followers was the *Sermon* 39 on *Catholic Spirit.* This is yet another non-theological factor in the Methodist ethos. Its use in motivating generations after generation of Methodist ecumenists is well-known and well-documented, but we can also notice that it has implications for the inter-faith movement. The central passage is:

> While he is steadily fixed in his religious principles, on what he believes to be the truth as it is in Jesus; while he firmly adheres to that worship of God which he judges to be the most acceptable in His sight, and while he is united in the tenderest and closest ties to one particular congregation - his heart is enlarged towards all mankind, those he knows and those he does not; he embraces with strong and cordial affection neighbours and strangers, friends and enemies. This is catholic or universal love. And he that has this is of a catholic spirit. For love alone gives the title to this character: catholic love is a catholic spirit.[128]

This love is as ever the constant theme of Wesleyanism, and has led many Methodists into the paths of inter-faith dialogue. From the days of James Hope Moulton and Edwin Smith on the British side, and E. Stanley Jones and Murray Titus in the American tradition, we can be thankful for Methodists whose hearts have been enlarged towards

---

[128] Sermon 39 *Catholic Spirit*, *Works*, Vol 2, p. 94.

all humankind, and who have taught Christians everywhere what it might mean to 'speak honourably ... of the work of God, by whomsoever he works, and kindly of his messengers.'[129]

---

[129] *Ibid.*

Chapter Five

Wesleyan Theology into the New Millennium

1. Caught up in the Missio Dei

One of the most powerful motifs in contemporary missiology is called in shorthand: the *missio Dei,* the mission of God. Partly derived from the theology of Karl Barth and partly as a result of the challenge of the post second world-war period as new churches began to emerge throughout the world, the *missio Dei* concept came to describe mission as the primary activity of God, lying at the heart of God's being. The twofold movement of the Father sending the Son and the Son sending the Spirit, must be expanded to include the third: the sending by the Triune God, Father, Son and Holy Spirit of the Church into the world. 'As the Father has sent me, so send I you.' Mission has no independent life of its own, and is in no way the property or prerogative of the Church. Only in the hands of the sending God can the Church become a missionary church. Only as it participates in the movement of God's love towards humankind can it fulfil its mission. Virtually all Christian traditions have taken this understanding to themselves: certainly member churches of the WCC, certainly in Vatican II circles in Roman Catholicism; certainly large elements within Evangelicalism.[130]

---

[130] For a fuller treatment of the *missio Dei* David Bosch, *op.cit.*, pp. 389-90.

But in one sense Methodists knew of the *missio Dei* from their beginnings. Martin Schmidt, the great Lutheran interpreter of Methodism, says of its founder.

> He was the first in the whole course of church history who realised that the task of Christendom in modern world is to be defined as mission. Here again Wesley took his cue from the missionary enterprise to the Gentiles in the early days of the church. Wesley went to Georgia expressly because he wanted to be a missionary to the American Indians. He wanted to be in a position to recover the original meaning and purpose of the New Testament, which he recognised as a missionary document. This insight is something of the highest importance. [131]

Three consequences (at least) followed. Wesley knew in his bones that only by being actually preached would the Word of God reveal its fullest meaning. Second, he was able to discern that he lived in a missionary situation: Europe was inhabited just as much as were the Americas by those who had never heard the Gospel. Third, he was set free as no other Anglican before him to question the nature of the parochial system and eventually the nature of the Episcopal system.

> I look upon the world as my parish; thus far. I mean that in whatever part of it I am, I judge it right and my bounden duty to declare unto all who are willing to hear it the glad tidings of salvation, This is the work I know God has called me to; and I am sure that his blessing attends it. [132]

---

[131] Martin Schmidt, 'Wesley's Place in Church History' in Kenneth Rowe (ed.), *The Place of Wesley in the Christian Tradition*, Scarecrow Press, 1976, p. 89.
[132] Letter to James Hervey, 1739.

His heirs have understood these things as well, and the sense of being caught up in God's mission has determined their view of the Church.

Thus in Wesleyan thinking the Church is not an integral part of the Gospel in the way it is for the Eastern Orthodox, the Roman Catholics, and for many Anglicans. We have never thought that Jesus came to found a church and to leave the church then to do his work. Much rather he came to declare the Kingdom of God. The order of thinking, we believe, goes: 'Kingdom then the World then the Church' rather than 'Kingdom then the Church then the World.' When the church and its interpretation of Christ's ordinances stood in the way of the provision of preachers and leaders for the American Methodist Conference in 1784, and John Wesley ordained his own superintendents (or bishops -- Francis Asbury and Thomas Coke), mission and kingdom took precedence over tradition, pastoral need was more urgent than catholicity, and evangelistic demands were of a higher priority than church order.[133] No wonder we have caused so much pain to our mother church with her greater sense of catholicity. A further consequence is that Methodist ecclesiological thinking is relatively rudimentary when compared with its missiology.

So from the beginning the focus of Christian witness lay beyond the boundaries of the church. Witness to transformative grace for Methodists has meant that nothing should stand in the way of the 'great salvation' promised to all people. God's mission of transformative grace can take up any Christian community or any Christian individual into God's ultimate purposes.

---

[133] 'What is the end of all ecclesiastical order? Is it not to brings souls from the power of Satan to God, and to build them up in His fear and love? Order is so far valuable as it answers these end; and if it answers them not it is nothing worth.' *Letter to John Smith*, June 25, 1746.

Because of this profound sense of being caught up in something that God is doing, and not we ourselves, Wesley and his followers have believed that inherited traditions and well-tried methods are strong enough and resilient enough to be put at risk for the sake of Gospel outreach. As Robert Cummings Neville has written of John Wesley and his movement:

> He was an Anglican and struggled all his life to remain loyal to that tradition. Yet he took the Gospel to people whose culture was not in tune with Anglican sensibilities. He modified liturgies, rephrased theologies, and with his brother invented a new hymnody to meet the needs of people who were not reached by his inherited unchanged traditions. When his movement in America lacked leadership, he took the step of ordaining leaders that by tradition, he could not do without being a bishop ... Wesley's emphasis on risking tradition for evangelical outreach is extremely important for these times of rapid change in Christianity. It is not surprising that Methodists were among the first to risk patriarchal traditions to bring women into positions of leadership. Nor is it surprising that Methodists risk their connexional systems to bring the gospel to foreign language communities, from the German communities of the nineteenth century to the Korean congregations of today. Nor is it surprising that Methodists have risked European forms of church life to embrace diversely indigenized church bodies around the world, as gathered in the World Methodist Council.[134]

We need just add the last word here that in Methodist thinking the church *happens* through the work of the Holy Spirit: When the Word comes with the power of the Spirit, renewing and revivifying the community, converting, justi-

---

[134]   *Truth and Tradition: A Conversation about the Future of United Methodist Theological Education*, Abingdon Press, 1995, p. 48.

fying, sanctifying sinful men and women and transforming their lives and their fellowship then there is church. It is then that they become a people 'called to love and praise.'

2. By Being Non-establishment

'But Wesley's real conversion was not Aldersgate: it was when he determined to break clean from culture-religion and freely to use field preaching to win followers on a voluntary basis.' So has written Franklin H. Littell, one of the most distinguished of American church historians. As a Methodist minister, he was invited in 1963 to ponder the future of the Wesleyan movement in an article in *The Christian Century.* [135] Writing against the specific background of the movement for civil rights, Littell laments, with telling examples, the conformity to the culture-religion of the USA, nurtured by the desire of Methodist leadership to be part of the establishment. For Littell, culture-religion is what he saw as a young Methodist youth leader in Germany in 1938, when, as he tells us, he met a German Methodist Bishop who assured him (in the days of 'Kristalnacht' and the Nuremberg rallies, that 'Hitler was God's man for Germany.' Littell writes:

> I want to be understood clearly in my reference to Bishop Melle. We are much too inclined to think of such things in individualistic terms, to resolve structural and historical issues by blaming individuals. Otto Melle was good man -- a pastor, a patriot, President of the German Temperance Movement (Blaue Kreuz), personally devout. And yet because his theology was defective -- individualistic, lacking a sound sense of social sin and evil, alienated rather than linked to Israel's pilgrimage through history --

---

[135] Later published in Kyle Hazelden and Martin E. Marty (eds.), *What's Ahead for the Churches*? Sheed and Ward, 1964, pp. 74-93: the quotation comes from p. 90.

he simply failed to perceive the true meaning of history and the true crisis of the age.[136]

This single example enables us to focus on the serious dangers in an 'establishment-mentality' and in the cultural-religious tendencies so often to be seen in Protestant mainstream denominations. Broadly speaking the peril here is to water down the claims of social discipleship lest any one be excluded from the church simply for holding the views of society all around. This is what a missiologist sees as accommodation and acculturation: bending the Gospel to suit the prevailing mores. In societies based upon the market economy or inherited class or caste systems, the challenges of Jesus are attenuated. Thus in Europe and North America a person may hold reactionary political or social views, or be committed to racist and sexist ideologies, or be known as a harsh and unscrupulous employer, but no formal complaint is ever made and no discipline is ever imposed. Rather it becomes more important to worry about individual misdemeanours, alcohol and drug abuse, sexual deviance, the wickedness of abortion and so on. But to go this way is to make Wesley's own fears about his movement come true:

> I am not afraid that the people called Methodists should ever cease to exist either in Europe or America. But I am afraid, lest they should only exist as a dead sect, having the form of religion, without the power. And this will undoubtedly be the case, unless they hold fast both the doctrine, spirit and the discipline with which they first set out.[137]

So Methodists need to remind themselves continually of the significance of 'field preaching' and its implications.

---

[136] In his art. 'United Methodism in a World of Religious Diversity', cited above, pp. 125-6.
[137] *Thoughts upon Methodism*, 1786.

Methodists are non-establishment people, volunteers in a free association that 'ever remembers' it was raised up 'to spread scriptural holiness throughout the land' (or in American tradition 'over these lands'). They need, especially in American Methodism (but abuses are not unknown in the British tradition) to remember why our ministers are itinerant.[138] In our beginnings, if a society resisted the counsel and standards of the church, it would be confronted by a much tougher and more experienced pastor the next time round. Today prophetic utterance and style can get a preacher moved on, and a more congenial and 'accommodating' parson is chosen in his or her place. Both traditions of Methodism fret over the logistics of itineracy but the principle lying behind it should not be abandoned. Itineracy is about discipling and nurture, not convenience and conviviality.

Discipling and nurture are the supreme matters for Methodist renewal. One anxiety always for a missiologist about Church Growth movements lies exactly here. Too great a desire for rapidly growing churches may lead to emphasising 'converts' rather than 'disciples.'[139] Even in New Testament language this is a false emphasis, for the 'Great Commission' in Matthew 28.18-20 plainly lays upon those who surrounded the Lord the injunction to 'disciple the nations ... teaching them to observe all that I have commanded you'. To be sure English translations often miss

---

[138] For North American discussions of the issues see Dennis E. Campbell, *The Yoke of Obedience*, Abingdon, 1988 and Donald E. Messier (ed.), *Send Me: The Itinerancy in Crisis,* Abingdon, 1991.

[139] I notice that Church of the Nazarene theologian Floyd Cunningham concurs: he writes, 'The zeal for making as many converts and of planting as many churches as possible has always been an essential part of the Christian mission at least as far as holiness churches are concerned; but it has been considered only one part of it. The overarching mission has been to see moral transformation, Christ-likeness reproduced in converts, and the kingdom of Christ come to fulfilment. Too often evangelical conversion has required no transformation of character, and relatively few changes in belief except about the necessity of accepting "Christ for one's own salvation", *op.cit,* p.202.

the point, for 'to disciple' is not really an English verb. They use some formulation like 'make disciples of the nations', which means to most readers, 'from out of the nations.' Large numbers of 'converts' was never Wesley's aim. He was vastly more concerned about their nurturing as disciples, for to win people without providing for them the means of grace was but 'to breed children for the Murderer.'[140] For this discipling the class meeting was his chosen instrument.[141] In it those beginners on the Christian road learned the fundamentals of Christian belief, the older ones continued to grow in grace and reinforce each other's witness and both, in Littell's phraseology, learned the 'separation which marks the Christian style of life from that affirmed by the spirit of the times.' To be sure there were reasons why the old class meeting fell into disuse, and it is perhaps impossible to re-instate it. But the principle remains untarnished. To win people without discipling them is worse than a waste of time; to disciple them is to form a great new apostolate, a people prepared to spread scriptural holiness through the world.

3. By Being Ecumenical

Because Methodists are committed to the 'Body of Christ' conception of the Church (British Methodists explicitly claim and cherish their place 'in the Holy Catholic Church, which is the Body of Christ'), they have never forgotten how to sing:

---

140   *Journal*, August 25, 1763, Wesley used this expression when travelling in Wales and found there so little fruit of the much-vaunted Welsh revival. 'How much preaching there has been for these past twenty years all over Pembrokeshire! But no *regular societies*, no discipline, no order or connection. And the consequence is that nine out of the ten once awakened are now faster asleep than ever.'(emphasis his) *Works*, Vol. 21, p. 424.

141   For recent research into this phenomenon, see David Lowes Watson, *The Early Class Meeting: Its Origins and Significance*, Discipleship Resources, 1985.

Christ from whom all blessings flow
Perfecting thy saints below;
Hear us, who thy nature share,
Who thy mystic body are.[142]

The sense of how shocking and disgraceful it is to live in the broken body of Christ is never wholly suppressed within the Wesleyan consciousness.[143] Divisions within Methodism have been particularly distressing, and Methodists were among the first to use the term ecumenical. The first Ecumenical Methodist Conference in 1881 was an attempt to heal the rifts of the Wesleyan movement (in 1881 there were ten separate Methodist denominations in the English tradition, eighteen in the American). Happily we have, under God, been able to heal many of these. The first nation-wide church union scheme this century, the United Church of Canada in 1925 included the Canadian Methodist Church; the British Methodists came together in 1932; there was a reunion of three Methodist Churches in the re-formed Methodist Episcopal Church in 1939; Methodists in South India joined the Church of South India in 1947. The World Methodist Council was formed in 1956 and the search for church unity goes on through it as well as through the World Council of Churches. But not only at the world level are Methodists involved: all national and regional dialogues have strong Methodist participation.

Methodists have gifts to bring to this ecumenical quest: their passionate distress about the brokenness of Christ's body, their profound historical experience of exclusion, the ways they do their theology, their formation in 'catholic

---

[142] *A Collection of Hymns for the Use of the People Called Methodists*, 1780, No 504, *Works*, Vol. 7, p. 693, *Hymns and Psalms*, No. 764.
[143] 'Above all beware of schism, of making a rent in the Church of Christ. Beware of everything tending thereto. Beware of a divisive spirit. Shun whatever has the least aspect that way.' *Cautions and Directions Given to the Greatest Professors within the Methodist Societies*, 1762.

spirit', their unbroken links with both Catholicism and the Reformation, their sense of the transitory nature of denominationality, their willingness to lose their identity in order to discover God's promises. This people goes on to sing in the same hymn:

> Love like death has all destroyed,
> Rendered all distinctions void;
> Names and sects and parties fall,
> Thou O Christ art all in all.[144]

This ending of names and sects and parties remains an eschatological hope, a vision for our pilgrimage. But it is undoubtedly the Wesleyan vision. Meanwhile we do our best. Albert Outler catches the vision of the best we can offer when he describes the calling of Methodism to be 'an evangelical order of witness and worship, discipline and nurture' within 'an encompassing environment of catholicity.'[145]

4. By Being Wesleyan

A community that ever remembers that it was raised up 'to spread Scriptural holiness', that knows its doctrinal standards, that sings its faith, that works in its relations with others on the basis of a mixture of practical common sense and catholic spirit, has a distinct contribution to make to the human community. Aware of the extraordinary nature of the grace-filled potentiality in every situation it will live close to its Lord bearing the marks of happiness and holiness and heaven.[146] Knowing from the depth of its heart that no one is unloved by God, it will renew its energies in serving the left-outs, the hungry ones, the despised of the

---

144   *Ibid*, p. 694.
145   *The Wesleyan Theological Heritage*, p. 226.
146   Albert Outler once counted fifty pairings of the words 'happiness' and 'holiness' in the writings of John Wesley.

earth. Knowing that every one is capable of transformation it will continue its dedicated ministries among the addicts and the abusers, the convicts and the criminals. Aware of the multiple ways in which God touches human lives it will be at the forefront of the ecumenical movement and the dialogue between people of different faith commitments.

Such renewal and rededication is dependent, under God, on the individuals who make up the Methodist movement. Some of us are cradle Methodists, born into this extraordinary movement of God without knowing quite what our inheritance is; others of us have found ourselves at home within this community, joining this people because of its differences from the Christianity in which we were nurtured; some of us, again, have found our way from no faith and false faith into the splendour of Christian obedience through the life and witness of this community. What is only implicit to us needs now to be made explicit. What we may have taken for granted needs to be raised to full consciousness. What we may have forgotten needs to remembered afresh. To these ends I make two suggestions. The first I borrow from William Abraham. Concerned lest those becoming members of the United Methodist Church are admitted without any challenge to confess 'the apostolic faith and the precious distinctive of our own tradition' he raises the possibility of asking the following questions: 'Will you receive the treasures of the apostolic faith as enshrined in the doctrines of the United Methodist Church?' and 'Will you, with us, seek to order your life by those doctrines as the Holy Spirit works in you and in to bring us to full maturity in Jesus Christ?' [147] Truly, some such questioning needs to be addressed, from time to time, to

---

[147] *Waking from Doctrinal Amnesia*, p. 102.

old as well as new members of all Methodist churches. My second suggestion is that the questions asked of ministers existing and potential (as for example in Britain: 'Do we continue to believe and preach our doctrines ...'[148]) should become rather less of a formality. We are living in a Wesleyan theological renaissance -- the scores of books and articles listed in the footnotes indicate this -- and our preachers and teachers should be sharing in this rebirth. The world Methodist community is full of educated and highly motivated lay people who would be enthralled by the riches being uncovered in this rediscovery of authentic Wesleyanism. But how shall they hear of them without their preachers and teachers first having drunk deeply of these wells?

So we come to an end. Methodist theology, I have argued, is a distinctive and classical theology. Lived out by faithful Methodist people it is a 'classical Christianity.' Its source and its inspiration is the living God whom we are called to love and praise.[149]

---

[148] Question 2 of the Synod Spring Meeting - Ministerial Session in the British Methodist Church.

[149] As this book goes to press, there comes to hand a quite superb volume from Theodore Runyon, *The New Creation: John Wesley's Theology Today,* Abingdon 1998. I can only quote the commendation from Juergen Moltmann: 'This is for me *the* Wesley book at the end of the century, with new perspectives for the next millennium.' Perhaps all Methodist preachers and teachers ought to test Moltmann's judgment as they come to answer the question: 'do we believe and preach our doctrines?'